日英対訳

アメリカ

Talking about USA in English

Q&A

山久瀬 洋二

IBCパブリッシング

まえがき

　アメリカは世界の実験場だとよくいわれます。

　もともと、先住民のネイティブ・アメリカンしか住んでいなかった広大な大地に、世界中から移民が集まり作り上げたのがアメリカという社会です。

　最初に、イギリスやオランダ、そしてスペインから、そしてアイルランドをはじめヨーロッパ各地から。同時にアフリカからは人々が奴隷として連れてこられました。その後、南米やアジア各地、さらにはロシアや中東と、今でも移民は世界中からアメリカに流れ込んでいます。

　こうした多彩な人種が一つの国に集まって、制度を作り、多様性を尊重して共存できるか。それが、アメリカが実験場だといわれる所以なのです。

　アメリカの社会は複雑です。一つ町の中に、そこに移住してきた人々のそれぞれの歴史があります。そこで先に定住した人々と、後発組の移住者との間の差別や偏見の歴史もあるかもしれません。宗教も複雑です。ヨーロッパでの迫害を逃れて移住したプロテスタント系の人々が、まずアメリカ社会での土台となりました。その後、イタリアやアイルランドなどからカトリック系の人々がやってきました。東欧やロシアからはユダヤ系の人々も多く海を渡りました。

　そしてその後、アジア各地、中東をはじめ、世界中から多様な背景をもった人々がアメリカに上陸しました。人種と宗教、さらにその背景にある文化。それらが地域地域に混在しています。

アメリカにやってきた人々は、辺境の地では命と財産を自衛しなければなりませんでした。イギリスから独立した時も、人々は銃をもって戦いました。そうした伝統がいま問われています。

　銃を保有することがよいことか、それとも犯罪の温床になる時代遅れの誤った考え方かという議論が沸騰しているのです。

　この議論は、アメリカ人一人一人が独立した個人として、自分のことは自分で決め、判断するという、過去を振り切って新大陸にやってきた移民ならではの「個人主義」という価値観のあり方をどう捉えるかという課題です。

　移民で大地を開拓してきた人々は、集団ではなく個人で判断し生き抜いてゆくことの大切さを植えつけられてきたのです。

　アメリカという社会を理解し、そこの政治や文化に接するには、こうした彼らの考え方をしっかりと心に留めておくことが大切です。

　今、アメリカは転換期にあります。こうした伝統的な価値観をめぐっても、新たに移民を受け入れ、外から来る人に寛容であるべきかどうか、大統領選挙などでも政策が分かれています。アメリカの古い伝統を守ってゆくのか、これからも常に新しい血が世界中から流れ込んで、アメリカという社会の脱皮を続けてゆくのか。それはアメリカだけではなく世界に大きな影響を与える決断であるといえましょう。

　本書を、そんなアメリカを知り、それを通して世界の未来を占うヒントとして参考にしていただければ幸いです。

2017年1月　山久瀬　洋二

目次

CONTENTS

まえがき 2

第1章　アメリカの大地と人 9

アメリカの国土 10

アメリカの地形と自然 14

アメリカの気候 24

アメリカ人 32

アメリカの地域性 62

◆コラム◆ アメリカの地域性と大統領選挙 74

第2章　アメリカの歴史と背景 75

アメリカの国歌と国旗 76

アメリカの歴史 80

アメリカの世論、アメリカ人気質 110

◆コラム◆ パールハーバーとアメリカ 118

第3章　アメリカの政治 119

アメリカの民主主義 120

アメリカの法体系と人権 136

アメリカの内政 150

Chapter 1 The Land of the United States of America and Its People 9

USA Territory 11

Geographical and Natural Features
    of the USA 15

The Climate of the USA 25

The People of America 33

The Differences in Regions in the USA 63

Chapter 2 History and Background of the USA 75

National Anthem and Flag 77

The History of the USA 81

USA Public Opinion and the American
    Disposition 111

Chapter 3 American Politics 119

American Democracy 121

The Judicial System and Human Rights ... 137

Domestic Affairs 151

アメリカの福祉と健康 158

アメリカの外交 162

アメリカの軍事と宇宙開発 176

◆コラム◆ ドナルド・トランプが大統領に選ばれて . . . 184

第4章　アメリカの経済活動 185

アメリカ経済の背景 186

アメリカの産業界 200

アメリカの経営と職場環境 214

◆コラム◆ アメリカの世界企業の強さとは 224

第5章　社会・生活 225

アメリカの生活環境 226

宗　教 232

アメリカの社会問題 242

家庭とコミュニティ 252

人と自然 260

あとがき　268

Welfare and Health 159

American Diplomacy. 163

American Military and
Space Development 177

Chapter **4** **The US Economy** 185

Background of the US Economy 187

US Industries. 201

American Management and Office
Environments. 215

Chapter **5** **Society—Life** 225

The American Living Environment 227

Religion 233

American Social Problems 243

Family and Community 253

People and Nature. 261

Chapter 1

The Land of the United States of America and Its People

第1章　アメリカの大地と人

アメリカの国土

Q アメリカはどれくらい大きな国なのですか？

国の面積		
1位	ロシア	17,098,242 km²
2位	カナダ	9,984,670 km²
3位	アメリカ	9,833,517 km²
4位	中国	9,596,961 km²
5位	ブラジル	8,514,877 km²
62位	日本	377,972 km²

983万3,517km²の国土を持つアメリカ。これは日本の約25倍の広さとなります。最も広大な州はアラスカ州で、151万8,875km²。また、アメリカ本土で最も大きな州はテキサス州で、69万2,141km²の面積（日本の約1.83倍）を有しています。

この広大な土地に日本の約2倍強の人々、すなわち3億2,500万人の人々が生活しているのです。

ニューヨークとサンフランシスコとを結ぶ高速道路80号線でアメリカを東から西まで車で横断すれば、約4,630kmの旅となります。普通、車で大陸を横断するには1週間は必要です。もし、飛行機で大陸を横断すれば、所要時間は6時間（西から東へ飛べば偏西風に乗って5時間）です。

時差は、東海岸と西海岸で3時間。従って、サンフランシスコのダウンタウンに人が出勤して来る頃には、ニューヨークは既にランチの時間というわけです。

Q アメリカの現在の領土はいつ決まったのですか？

アメリカは50の州からなる国家です。50州の中

USA Territory

Q How large is the USA?

The total land area of the USA is 9,833,517 km^2, 25 times as much as Japan. The largest state is Alaska, which is 1,518,875 km^2, but the largest of the 48 contiguous states is Texas, which is 692,141 km^2 (1.83 times larger than Japan).

This vast land is inhabited by 325 million people, a number which is just over twice Japan's population.

Driving east to west on Interstate 80, which connects New York and San Francisco, the trip is 4,630 km. It takes a week to cross the continent by car. The same trip takes 6 hours by plane, and one hour less flying west to east with the prevailing westerly winds.

There is a 3-hour time difference between the East and West Coasts. This means that when commuters arrive at work in downtown San Francisco, New Yorkers are already having lunch.

Q When did USA territory gain its present form?

The United States of America is composed of fifty

で最後に州となったのはハワイで、1959年のことでした。

東部の13州がイギリスからの独立を宣言したのが1776年。そして、ミシシッピ川流域以西の広大な平原をフランスから購入したのが1803年でした。

また、現在のテキサス州は、もともとメキシコの領土でした。それをメキシコとの戦争の末に正式に獲得したのが1845年。さらに、カリフォルニアは1850年にアメリカの州となりました。

アメリカ本土の領土が確定したのは、1853年にメキシコから、大陸横断鉄道の建設を目的として、現在のアリゾナとニューメキシコにまたがる地域を約1,000万ドルで購入したときです。また、1867年にはアラスカをわずか720万ドルでロシアから購入しました。

こうした事実は、アメリカが1つの国家でありながら、その起こりも背景も異なる様々な州の寄り合い所帯であることを意味しています。それぞれの州はそうした背景の違いから、自らの独自のカラーを活かした政治や経済活動を目指しているところが多く、それが、アメリカならではの多様な地域性を生み出しているのです。

1845年までメキシコが実行支配していた地域

Q アメリカ本土以外にどのような地域がアメリカを構成しているのですか？

アメリカ本土以外で、アメリカの州となってい

states. The most recent addition was Hawaii, which became a state in 1959.

The thirteen eastern states declared independence from Great Britain in 1776. In 1803, the vast prairie lands west of the Mississippi River were purchased from France.

The state of Texas, on the other hand, originally belonged to Mexico. The USA attained this state in a war with Mexico in 1845. California became a state in 1850.

The territory of mainland USA was fixed definitively when the region straddling present-day Arizona and New Mexico was purchased from Mexico in 1853 for $10 million, in order to construct the transcontinental railway. Alaska was purchased from Russia for only $7.2 million in 1867.

As these facts show, the USA is a country that consists of various states, each with its own origins and background. As a consequence, many states have developed their own unique governments and economic activities, which all contribute to the diversity from region to region.

Q What are the areas, besides the 48 contiguous states, that compose the USA?

There are two other states besides the 48 contiguous

スペイン領だった頃の名残、プエルトリコのモーロ要塞

るのはハワイとアラスカです。また、アメリカは多くの島を領有しています。代表的なのが、カリブ海に浮かぶプエルトリコで、プエルトリコは州に準ずる地域として、そこに住む人々にはアメリカ人と同じ市民権が与えられています。そのほか、プエルトリコの東にあるバージン諸島の一部や、アラスカから西に伸びるアリューシャン列島の大部分もアメリカ領です。また、太平洋に浮かぶグアムやサイパンなどの島々で知られるマリアナ諸島やその南のマーシャル諸島なども、第2次世界大戦以来アメリカが管理しています。

アメリカの地形と自然

Q アメリカの自然の特徴はどのようになっているのですか？

　一般的にいって、東海岸はなだらかな丘陵地が多く、四季の変化が際立っています。南部の夏は暑く、南へ行けば亜熱帯性の植物をよく見かけます。アメリカの中部（ミッドウエスト）は、もともとは広大な草原地帯でしたが、現在では開墾され農地になっています。中西部の北側は森や湖が多く、気候は冬は厳しく、夏は穏やかです。

states: Hawaii and Alaska. The USA also possesses many islands. The largest is Puerto Rico in the Caribbean Sea, which is treated similarly to a state, and whose residents have US citizenship. Some parts of the Virgin Islands to the east of Puerto Rico, and most of the Aleutian Islands to the west of Alaska, are American territories. The Mariana Islands, the largest of which are Guam and Saipan, and the Marshall Islands to the south of the Marianas, have been under the trust of the USA since WWII.

Geographical and Natural Features of the USA

Q What are the USA's natural features?

Generally speaking, the East Coast is characterized by gently sloping hills and distinct changes of season. The South has hot summers, and the farther south one goes, the more subtropical plants one will see. The central part of the USA (the Midwest) was originally a vast sweep of prairies, but it has now been made into farmland. To the north of the Midwest are many

左：コロラド州から見るロッキー山脈
右：アメリカ大陸西部を北西から南東に走る大山脈（ロッキー山脈）

　ミッドウエストからさらに西に行き、ロッキー山脈を越えれば、広大な砂漠地帯が広がります。特にアリゾナなどの南部の砂漠では、大きなサボテンをみかけ、炎暑は時には人の命を奪うほどです。逆に西部でも北側は冬が厳しく、険しい山があちこちにあります。

　西海岸の気候は一様に温暖です。ところどころ山が海岸線まで迫り、北部は杉林が多く、カリフォルニア州中部以南は、松や杉林のほかに、草原やステップ、ところによっては砂漠が海辺近くまで続いているところもあります。

Q　アメリカにはどんな山がありますか？

　アメリカ合衆国には東部と西部とに2つの背骨（山脈）があります。その昔、ヨーロッパから入植してきた人々が、東海岸から内陸へと旅して最初にぶつかったのが、東部を南北に貫くアパラチア山脈とそこに広がる深い森と谷でした。

forests and lakes, and the climate is extremely cold in the winter and mild in the summer.

A vast desert area extends west of the Midwest across the Rocky Mountains. In the southern part of the desert, in Arizona, huge cacti grow, and the heat can be so extreme that fatalities occur. The northern part of the West, on the other hand, has extremely cold winters and steep mountains.

On the West Coast, the climate is generally mild. Mountains stretch down almost to the coastline in places. There are cedar forests in the north, and pines and cedars from the middle to the south of California, as well as prairies and steppes. In some areas, the desert almost reaches the coast.

Q What kind of mountain ranges does the USA have?

The US has two "backbones," or mountain ridges, in the East and the West. In early times, when European settlers traveled inland from the East Coast, they found their passage impeded first by the Appalachian Mountains, which run north to south, then by deep

深い森が続くアパラチア山脈

アパラチア山脈を越えれば、その先はミッドウエスト（中西部）と呼ばれる大平原。そのはるか彼方には、高く険しいロッキー山脈が横たわっています。この大山脈を越えて砂漠地帯をさらに西に行けば、北はカスケード山脈、南はシエラ・ネバダ山脈といったロッキーに勝るとも劣らない山脈が見えてきます。その尾根を越えれば、そこはもう太平洋です。

アメリカの高山はアラスカに集中しています。特にマッキンレー山は標高6,194m（世界ランキング35位）で、北米一の高さがあります。ちなみに、アメリカの本土で最も高い山はカリフォルニア州にあるホイットニー山（4,418m）です。

Q 五大湖とはどのような湖ですか？

五大湖は氷河時代の氷が溶けて湖になったものです。それは、アメリカとカナダとの国境に房のように集まる5つの巨大な湖で、淡水湖群としては世界最大の規模を有しています。西はミネソタ州、東はニューヨーク州にまたがっています。

西から順にスペリオル、ミシガン、ヒューロン、エリー、そしてオンタリオの順に並んでいます。特にスペリオル湖は、カスピ海についで世界で2番目の湖沼面積があり、それは日本の本州の3分の

forests and valleys.

Beyond Appalachia lies the plains of the Midwest. At the far end of the plains run the steep Rocky Mountains. Beyond the Rockies, going further west into the desert, one meets the Cascade Range in the north and the Sierra Nevada Range in the south, both as high as the Rockies. Beyond those ranges lies the Pacific Ocean.

The highest mountains in the US is in Alaska. Mt. McKinley, at 6,194 m above sea level, is the highest mountain in North America (ranked 35th in the world). The highest mountain in the 48 contiguous states is Mt. Whitney in California, at 4,418 m.

Q What kind of lakes are the Great Lakes?

These five huge lakes gathered in a cluster at the US-Canada border were formed when the ice of the Ice Age melted. They are the largest group of fresh-water lakes in the world, extending from the state of Minnesota in the West to the state of New York in the East.

Their names are, from west to east, Lake Superior, Michigan, Huron, Erie and Ontario. Lake Superior is the second largest lake in the world next to the Caspian Sea. At 82,414 km^2 it is one-third the size of Japan's

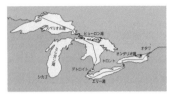
五大湖分布図

1強の広さ（8万2,414km^2）に相当します。さらに、ヒューロン湖が世界第5位で、ミシガン湖が6位、エリー湖とオンタリオ湖がそれぞれ11位と15位と続いています。

　五大湖の全ての湖は、直接、あるいは川などを通して繋がっていて、さらに最も東にあるオンタリオ湖からは、セントローレンス川が大西洋まで伸びています。また、エリー湖周辺からは、運河と川を経由して、ニューヨークまで船で物を運ぶことが可能で、南へ下ればミシシッピ川を経由してメキシコ湾へと抜けることもできます。

　こうした背景から、五大湖周辺は交通の要衝として早くから開拓され、バッファローやデトロイト、そしてシカゴといった大都市が生まれ、19世紀末以降、アメリカの物流や生産拠点の1つとして機能してきたのです。

Q　ミシシッピ川とはどんな川ですか？

　ミシシッピ川が暴れ出すと、日本のスーパーマーケットで肉の値段が上がるといわれています。なぜでしょう。実はこの川の周辺には、日本の家畜の飼料となるとうもろこしが生産されているコーン・フィールドが広がっているのです。最近では、事情が変わってきており、日本もアメリカ以外の国々から肉の輸入を行っています。

Honshu Island. Lake Huron is the fifth largest in the world, Lake Michigan the sixth, and Lake Erie and Ontario the eleventh and fifteenth.

All the Great Lakes are connected with each other, either directly or indirectly via rivers. From Lake Ontario, which is the easternmost body of water, the St. Lawrence River extends into the Atlantic Ocean. From Lake Erie it is possible to transport goods to New York via rivers and canals. It is possible to go all the way down to the Gulf of Mexico via the Mississippi River.

The regions around the Great Lakes were thus an important hub of transportation from early times. Big cities like Buffalo, Detroit, and Chicago from the end of the 19th century onwards functioned as distribution and manufacturing centers for the USA.

Q What kind of river is the Mississippi?

It is said that when the Mississippi River rages, the cost of meat in Japanese supermarkets goes up. Why? Because the corn fields stretching along the river produce cornfeed for Japanese livestock. This has changed in recent years as Japan has diversified its meat imports from other countries.

北はカナダに近いミネソタの湖沼地帯に源を発し、メキシコ湾に流れ出るミシシッピ川。ミシシッピとは、チペワ・インディアンの言葉で「父なる川(Father of the Waters)」を意味しています。アメリカはこの川によって東西に二分されています。西部開拓が盛んに行われていた頃は、ミシシッピ川流域までは、容易に東海岸から移動することができました。そして、この川を越えると、いよいよ西部への旅となるのです。

　19世紀、川には蒸気船が行き来し、それに乗って物資や人が往来しました。周辺には肥沃な平原が広がり、北はとうもろこし畑、南部へ下ると綿畑、そして西へ行けばグレート・プレーンと呼ばれる牧草地帯、穀倉地帯がどこまでも

ミシシッピ川を行き来する蒸気船(ニューオーリンズ付近)

続いています。今でも、ミシシッピ川とその支流によって形成されるミシシッピ川水系の貨物輸送量は全米の水運量の6割近くを占め、アメリカの大地を貫く大動脈として機能しているのです。

　ミシシッピ川の最大の支流であるミズーリ川と、その合流点から南の本流の長さを加えた総延長は6,210km。これは、ナイル川、そしてアマゾン川、揚子江に次いで世界第4位の長さとなります。

Q　アメリカにはどんな国立公園があるのですか？

　現在アメリカには59の国立公園(ナショナルパーク)があります。ナショナルパークとは、特に際立っ

The Mississippi flows down from the lake areas in Minnesota into the Gulf of Mexico. The word Mississippi means "Father of the Waters" in the Native American Chippewa language, and the USA is divided into east and west by this river. In the frontier period, it was relatively easy to travel from the East Coast as far as the river. To "go west" actually meant to travel beyond it.

In the nineteenth century, steamboats plied the river, carrying goods and people. On either side lie stretches of fertile plains—corn fields in the north, cotton fields in the south. To the west there are long stretches of pastures and granaries. The freight volume transported along the Mississippi and its tributaries amounts to almost 60% of total water transport in the USA. The Mississippi River actually functions as a main artery supplying the American Continent.

The total length of the Mississippi, including its longest tributary, the Missouri, is 6,210 km. This makes it the fourth longest river in the world, after the Nile, the Amazon, and the Chang Jiang.

Q What kind of national parks does the USA have?

The USA has 59 national parks. Areas with remarkable natural scenery and views or resources that are

た自然や景観、そして科学的、地質学的、あるいは生物学的に貴重な資源とみなされる場所を連邦政府の管理下において保護し、一般に開放しているものです。最も早くナショナルパークに指定されたのは、ワイオミング州とモンタナ州、アイダホ州にまたがるイエローストーン・ナショナルパークで、1872年のことでした。

アメリカのナショナルパークの特徴は、その規模の大きさではないでしょうか。総延長が450kmにも及ぶ巨大な谷をそっくりナショナルパークに指定したグランド・キャニオンや、山梨県が2つすっぽりと入ってしまうイエローストーンなどはその代表的な例で、多くの人々は休暇を利用して、何日もかけてその雄大な自然を楽しんでいます。

世界初の国立公園、イエローストーン・ナショナルパーク

アメリカの気候

Q アメリカの気候の特徴とはどのようなものですか？

広大なアメリカにはほとんど全ての気候帯があります。アメリカ本土でみるならば、最も暑い地域はアリゾナからネバダ南部、そしてカリフォルニア内陸部に至る砂漠地帯で、時には摂氏50度を超える高温になることもあり、1913年にはカリ

scientifically, geologically, or biologically invaluable are designated as national parks, and are protected under the management of the federal government. These parks are open to the public. The first national park was designated in 1872. It was Yellowstone National Park, which extends over the states of Wyoming, Montana, and Idaho.

The most notable characteristic of American national parks is their huge scale. The Grand Canyon has a total length of 450 km; Yellowstone is as large as two Yamanashi prefectures. People often spend several days at a time at these parks, enjoying the vastness of nature during their vacations.

The Climate of the USA

Q What are the characteristics of the American climate?

The USA comprises a vast area of land, so almost every kind of climate can be observed. Among the 48 contiguous states, the hottest zone is the desert area that stretches across Arizona, southern Nevada, and inland California, where the temperature sometimes rises to

フォルニア州のデスバレーで57度を記録しています。

逆に寒冷地といえば、特にモンタナ州からミネソタ州にかけてのカナダとの国境地帯が有名です。1954年にモンタナ州でマイナス56.5度まで温度が下がったという記録が残っています。

Q 竜巻は本当にあちこちで起こるのですか？

竜巻はアメリカ本土のほとんどの地域で起きています。それは特に春から夏にかけての雷を伴った強い嵐の時などに起こりがちで、時には数百人の死者を出すほどに大きな被害を出すこともあるため、何とか竜巻の発生を正確に予測できないかと、気象学者たちが研究を続けています。

特に竜巻の多い地域は、カンザス州、ネブラスカ州、オクラホマ州、テキサス州といったアメリカ内陸部で、これらの州とその周辺はトルネード・アレー(竜巻銀座)と呼ばれています。アメリカで最も竜巻が多いのはテキサス州で、毎年、平均して153の竜巻が発生しています。こうした地域ではビルなどに竜巻の時に避難する場所についての案内板があって、いざというときにはビルの中心部の構造のしっかりした所に退避するのです。

フロリダで起きた竜巻

over 50°C. In 1913, a temperature of 57°C was recorded in California's Death Valley.

The coldest zone is the USA-Canada border from Montana to Minnesota. Montana holds the record −56.5°C in 1954.

Q Do tornadoes really occur in various places?

Tornadoes have been known to occur almost everywhere in the USA. They are most likely to occur during the strong thunderstorms from spring to summer. Since tornadoes can cause serious damage and hundreds of fatalities, meteorologists continue to research how to accurately predict their occurrence.

Tornadoes occur particularly in inland areas like Kansas, Nebraska, Oklahoma, or Texas. These states are known collectively as "Tornado Alley." An average of 153 tornadoes touch down in Texas each year, making it the state with the most tornadoes in the US. These regions have instruction billboards showing people specific buildings to escape to in the case of a tornado. Buildings with sturdy central structures make safe evacuation sites.

Q　アメリカでは日本のように地震があるのですか？

　　太平洋とアメリカ大陸のプレートがぶつかる950kmに及ぶサン・アンドレアスなどの断層の周辺、すなわち西海岸がアメリカで最も地震の多いところです。

ロマ・プリータ地震での被害

　　よく知られているのが、1906年にサンフランシスコを襲ったもので、レクタースケールでマグニチュード8.3、478人の死者の他に、火事によって町の多くが焼失しました。その後1989年にもワールドシリーズに沸くサンフランシスコをまたも地震が襲いました。ロマ・プリータと呼ばれるこの大地震では、高速道路が寸断されるなどの被害が出たのです。

　　ではその他の所は全く安全かというと決してそんなことはありません。現に、サウス・カロライナ州の古都チャールストンは、1886年にマグニチュード7.7の地震に見舞われていますし、1811年にはアメリカのど真ん中のミズーリ州で大地震が起きています。さらに最近では、マグニチュード5.8の地震が、ワシントンD.C.からそう遠くないところで起き、ワシントン・モニュメントにもダメージがありました。

バージニア地震
2011年8月、バージニア州リッチモンドを震源とする大規模地震

Q　ハリケーンって台風とどこが違うのですか？

　　ハリケーンは大西洋で発生し、夏から秋にかけてアメリカの東海岸を襲う強い熱帯低気圧のこと

Q Does the USA have earthquakes like Japan?

Earthquakes take place mostly on the West Coast, around the San Andreas fault, which extends for 950 km where the Pacific and the American Continental tectonic plates meet.

The San Francisco earthquake of 1906 is particularly well known. It measured 8.3 on the Richter scale, caused 478 deaths, and engulfed most of the city in fire. Another earthquake hit San Francisco in 1989, just when the city was caught up in the excitement of the Superbowl, the final game in the season for American football. That quake, the Loma Prieta, was so violent it caused freeways to snap into two.

But other areas are not necessarily any safer. Charleston, the old capital of South Carolina, was hit by an earthquake of 7.7 magnitude in 1886. In 1811, a large earthquake was recorded in Missouri, the central part of the USA. More recently, an earthquake measuring 5.8 on the Richter scale not far from Washington, D.C., even damaged the famous Washington Monument.

Q How is a hurricane different from a typhoon?

Hurricanes are generated over the Atlantic Ocean. They are intense tropical depressions that attack the East

です。アメリカ版台風と思っていただいて結構です。台風銀座ならぬハリケーン銀座は、大西洋に面したフロリダからノース・カロライナ州にかけての沿岸地方と、メキシコ湾に面したテキサスからフロリダにかけての一帯です。

　1900年の8月末から9月にテキサスのガルベストンを襲ったハリケーンで6,000人を超える死者が出たのが、過去にハリケーンが最も暴れ回った記録です。2005年の8月末には、ハリケーン・カトリーナが、ルイジアナ州、ミシシッピ州、アラバマ州、そしてフロリダ州を襲いました。さらに最近では、2012年の10月にハリケーン・サンディが発生し、24の州に被害を与えました。被害の総額は70億ドルともいわれ、ニューヨーク市では地下鉄まで洪水で水浸しになったのです。
　ところで、昔はハリケーンのニックネームには女性の名前が付けられていました。これは、すぐ感情的になって、ヒステリーを起こすという女性に対するステレオタイプなイメージによるものですが、これは女性を差別するものということで、最近では、男性の名前も付けられるようになりました。社会の変化が、ハリケーンにも影響を与えたというわけです。

Coast from summer into autumn. The hurricane is, so to speak, an American typhoon. The areas that are most frequently hit are known as Hurricane Alleys. They consist of the coastal regions from Florida to North Carolina on the Atlantic, and from Texas to Florida on the Gulf of Mexico.

The most violent hurricane ever recorded was the one that attacked Galveston, Texas, at the end of August and into September in 1900: more than 6,000 people were killed. At the end of August in 2005, Louisiana, Mississippi, Alabama, and Florida was hit by Hurricane Katrina. More recently, the powerful Hurricane Sandy in October, 2012, impacted 24 states and did over $70 billion of damage, even flooding the subways in New York City.

Incidentally, in the past hurricanes were given women's names, a practice that derived from the stereotyped idea that women easily become emotional and hysterical. These days, men's names are also used to avoid gender discrimination. Thus, even the naming of hurricanes has been influenced by social change.

アメリカ人

Q アメリカの人口はどのように推移していったのですか？

アメリカの人口が3億を超えたのは2006年のことでした。現在（2016年）、その数は約3億2,500万人です。

アメリカに本格的に人が入植しはじめたのは、17世紀前半（1620年前後）でした。当時、アメリカで生活をしていたのはネイティブ・アメリカンを除くと、たった2,300人だったといわれています。それが独立戦争の頃（1770年代）には約214万人、19世紀初頭には約530万人と増え続けました。20世紀の初めには7,600万人となり、1920年の国勢調査で初めて人口が1億人を突破しました。そうです。300年という短期間に、これだけの人が海を越えてアメリカに移住し、増えていったのです。2050年にはアメリカの人口は4億人以上になるのではといわれています。

アメリカ独立戦争
1775年〜1783年。アメリカの13の植民地がイギリスから独立しようとした戦争。

Q 時代と共にどのような人たちがヨーロッパから移住してきたのですか？

アメリカはその起こりから、世界中からの移民を受け入れて大きくなった国です。その前提は現在まで変わることなく維持されてきました。

The People of America

Q How has the American population changed?

The American population topped the 300 million mark in 2006. Currently the figure is 325 million.

When people started settling in America on a large scale in the early seventeenth century (from 1620 onwards), it is said that only 2,300 people not native to the continent inhabited America. By the Civil War (1770) the population had grown to 2.14 million, and by the beginning of the nineteenth century, 5.3 million. By the beginning of the twentieth century, it had reached 76 million—and the 1920 census exceeded 100 million. In just three hundred years, the number of people who had immigrated to the USA and multiplied there had reached huge proportions. The population is expected to exceed 400 million in 2050.

Q What kinds of people emigrated to the USA from Europe?

From the start, the USA has accepted immigrants from all over the world and has expanded accordingly. That principle has remained the same over the years until now.

最初はイギリスやオランダ、そしてスペイン系の人々が黒人の奴隷と共にやってきました。次にアイルランド、ドイツ、イタリア、さらには東欧やロシアからユダヤ系の人々を交えた多くの人がやってきました。

　初期の人々は、宗教上の理由から移民し、生活を立てていこうという入植者でした。彼らの多くは、アメリカを信仰の自由のある新天地として、神が与えてくれた土地だと確信し開墾を続けました。また、新大陸でとれる毛皮などをヨーロッパに売ったりする商人も多く海を渡ってきました。

エリス島の初代移民局。大西洋を渡った多くの移民がこの島からアメリカに入国した

　それが、19世紀の中頃から、ヨーロッパでの貧困や迫害に追われるいわゆる経済移民、政治移民が増えるようになったのです。例えば、1846年にアイルランドで起きたじゃがいもの大飢饉で、飢えと貧困にあえぐアイルランドの人々が大挙して東海岸に流れ着きました。

　続いて、ヨーロッパでの政治不安によってドイツからの移民が押し寄せました。そして19世紀の終わりになると、ロシアや東欧での迫害を逃れて多くのユダヤ人がやって来ます。さらには季節労働者としてイタリア人がアメリカに押し寄せ、都市部の人口は瞬く間に膨れ上がりました。また、多少経済的に余裕のある移民は内陸部に入っていったので、地方もどんどん開発されていくことになります。

The first to come were the British, Dutch, and Spanish, who also brought their Black slaves. Next came the Irish, Germans, and Italians, followed by Jews from Russia and Eastern Europe.

The early settlers were people who had come over for religious regions, in order to make a living. Many of them thought of America as a "new world," a land God had given them to develop. There were also many fur merchants who came to America to export fur to Europe.

After the mid-nineteenth century, the number of immigrants seeking refuge for economic or political reasons such as poverty or persecution increased. For example, the great potato famine in Ireland in 1846 brought many hungry and poor Irish over to the East Coast.

The next wave of immigrants consisted of people from Germany, driven by fear of the political situation. From the end of the nineteenth century many Jews fled from Russia and Eastern Europe to avoid persecution. Italians also came as seasonal workers. The city populations quickly swelled with their numbers. Immigrants who had savings moved inland to develop the countryside.

ここ2、30年は、ヨーロッパからの移民は減り、代わってラテン・アメリカ、アフリカ、そしてアジア地域からの移民が顕著になっています。

Q 「アジア系のパワー」とはどのような現象を指すのですか？

アメリカに最初に移住してきたアジアの人々は、中国人でした。19世紀半ばのゴールドラッシュの頃に最初の中国人が西海岸に上陸し、下働きや鉱山労働、大陸横断鉄道の労働者として働きました。その後日系人が農業労働者としてハワイや西海岸に移住します。

鉄道労働者として働く中国人移民たち。
1863年〜1869年頃

しかし、アジアからの移民が増加し、古くから居住していた白人の職域を脅かすにつれ、日本人や中国人に対する排斥運動が起き、それが日本や中国からの移民を制限する法律の制定へと繋がっていきました。結局、アジアからの移民は、こうした法律が1960年代に廃止されるまで横這いの状態でした。

しかし、近年になって、新たなアジア系移民の流入が始まりました。それは香港や台湾、あるいは中国本土からの中国系移民、韓国系、それにベトナムをはじめとした東南アジア、さらにはインドやバングラデシュからの人々です。彼らは、

In recent decades immigration from Europe has decreased but there has been a dramatic increase in immigrants arriving from Latin America, Africa, and parts of Asia.

Q What phenomenon does the term "Asian Power" refer to?

The first Asian immigrants to the USA were Chinese. They came to the West Coast in the mid-nineteenth century during the time of the Gold Rush. They worked as servants, miners, and tracklayers in railway construction. Later, the Japanese immigrated into Hawaii and the West Coast as farmers.

As Asian immigrants increased, threatening the occupations of the whites who had long resided in those areas, anti-Japanese and anti-Chinese movements formed, leading to the establishment of a law to limit immigration from Japan and China. Immigration from Asia remained at the same low level until the law was abolished in 1960s.

Recent years have seen a new influx of Asian immigrants. It includes Chinese from Hong Kong, Taiwan and mainland China, Koreans, Southeast Asians such as Vietnamese, and immigrants from India and Bangladesh. They pour into East and West Coast cities.

ニューヨークや西海岸の都市部などへどんどん進出し、例えばニューヨークのチャイナタウンでは、40万人もの中国や他のアジアからの人々が生活をしています。

ここ2、30年で彼らはどんどんアメリカ社会に進出し、アメリカにおける新しい、しかも強力なパワーとして注目されてきたのです。

Q 現在アメリカはどのような人によって構成されている国なのですか？

アメリカには世界中の人が生活しているといっても差し支えありません。

面白いことに中西部の都市部にはエチオピアから来たタクシーの運転手さんがたくさんいます。また、テキサス州のメキシコ湾岸にはベトナム人の漁師さんが目立ちます。サンフランシスコとニューヨークには、大規模なチャイナタウンがあります。

カリフォルニア州の南部にはメキシコ系や中南米の人々がどんどん入ってきて、中には違法入国者も多いので移民局が神経を尖らせ、政治的な議論の場や、大統領候補討論会での熾烈なトピックになるほどなのです。しかし、その移民局の係員の多くもメキシコ系だったりアジア系だったりしています。

アメリカはますます多様に、そして多彩になっ

There are, for example, as many as 400,000 Chinese and other Asians living in Greater New York City.

Over the decades they lost no time in making inroads into American society and attracting attention as a new, strong power in the USA.

Q What is the current ethnic make-up of the USA population?

It is fair to say that the USA is inhabited by people from all over the world.

Interestingly, many of the cab drivers in Midwestern cities are Ethiopian. On the coast of the Gulf of Mexico in Texas, on the other hand, one can see many Vietnamese fishermen. San Francisco and New York both have extensive Chinatowns.

Mexicans and Central Americans are also pouring into Southern California. Many of them are "illegal aliens," and the source of headaches for immigration officials even becoming a hot topic in political discussions and presidential debates. However, many of the officers themselves are also immigrants from Mexico or Asia.

America is becoming increasingly diversified and

てきています。シリコンバレーのある会社では、ロシアやインドなどからきた技術者の数が、従来のアメリカ人の数を上回っています。現在、アメリカに住む全人口のうち、海外で生まれた移民1世の人の比率は12.1％となっています。2010年の国勢調査では、白人系以外の人が2050年までには白人系人口を上回るとしています。

こうした現象の中、従来のアメリカのアイデンティティがなくなることを恐れている人も多く、そうした人々は移民の流入を防ぐ強い法律や、違法にアメリカに入国してきた移民たちを国外退去させることを望んでいます。しかし、世界に紛争や貧困や政治的な抑圧がある限り、そしてアメリカに夢と豊かさと自由がある限り、人々は新大陸に船出し続けるのではないでしょうか。

Q 白人とはどういう人たちのことですか？

出自別アメリカ人構成 (2010年度)
1位 ドイツ系
2位 アフリカ系
3位 アイルランド系
4位 メキシコ系
5位 イングランド系
6位 アメリカ系
7位 イタリア系
8位 ポーランド系
9位 フランス系
10位 スコットランド系

アメリカで、一口に白人といっても、彼らのルーツは様々で、ヨーロッパ各地にその出身をみることができます。2010年の国勢調査の結果によれば、白人の中で最も多いのはドイツ系の人々で4,280万人、次いでアイルランド系の3,050万人、そして第3位がイギリス系で2,450万人、次がイタリア系の1,560万人という順でした。

白人といわれる人々の宗教的な背景もまちまち

colorful. In some companies in Silicon Valley, engineers from countries such as Russia and India exceed the number of US engineers. At present, the number of first-generation Americans born out of the USA is 12.1% of the total population. According to the 2010 US Census, the non-white population will exceed the white by the year 2050.

With all these changes, many people worry that the USA will lose its traditional identity. These people demand stricter laws to curb the influx of immigrants, or threaten to deport immigrants found to have entered the U.S. illegally. However, as long as conflict, poverty, and political oppression exist in the world, and as long as America offers the dream of affluence and freedom, people will continue to set out for the New World.

Q What kind of people make up the white population in America?

The white population in the USA originates from various places in Europe. According to the 2010 census, the largest segment is from Germany, at 42.8 million. These are followed by the Irish, at 30.5 million. Those from England number 24.5 million, and those from Italy, 15.6 million.

The religious background of the white population

です。ドイツ系とイギリス系の人々はいわゆるプロテスタントの背景を持つ人が多く、それに対してアイルランドやイタリアからきた人々は多くがカトリックです。例えば、同じ白人系でも、その中にはユダヤ系の人々もかなりいて、彼らの多くは異なった宗教や風習を維持しています。

890万ほどといわれるポーランド系の人々の多くはシカゴに住んでいます。ワルシャワを除けば、これほどポーランド人が集中しているところはありません。

アメリカ社会に広くとけ込んでいるアイルランド系の人々でも、あまりにも貧しかったため、他の白人グループから差別され、「アイルランド人はお断り」と書かれた求人広告が掲載された時代もありました。彼らはアイルランドがイギリスの植民地であったころに、貧困とイギリスの圧政に苦しんで海を渡ってきた人々が多く、同じくカトリック系の移民であるイタリア系の人々と同様、アメリカ社会の底辺から徐々に這い上がり、苦労の末成功を勝ち得た人々です。

Q　ワスプとはどのような人たちのことですか？

ワスプ（WASP）とは、ホワイト・アングロサクソン・プロテスタントの略です。彼らはアメリカの独立以前から新大陸に移住してきていた、特にニューイングランド地方に住んでいるか、そこの出身のイ

varies as well: German and British descendants are typically Protestant, while Irish and Italian are typically Catholic. But there are many other religions besides Christianity. For example, there are also Jews, with different cultural traditions.

Much of the Polish population (8.9 million in total) is concentrated in Chicago. In no other city in the world except Warsaw can one see so many Polish residents living together.

Descendants of Irish immigrants are now widely integrated into American society. Once, however, they were so poor that they suffered discrimination from other white groups. At one time it was common to see "No Irish" printed in many classified advertisements in newspapers. Many Irish immigrants originally fled poverty and the oppressive political situation in Ireland when it was a British colony. Like the Italians, who are also Catholic, they entered American society at the lowest level and endured hardships to gain success.

Q Who does the word "WASP" refer to?

WASP is a slang abbreviation for White Anglo-Saxon Protestant, a phrase that refers to the descendants of the British who came to America, lived in New England, and played a leading role in the history of American

メイフラワー号船内のピューリタンたちの様子。アメリカに渡り、ニューイングランドを開拓した

ギリス系の人々のことで、アメリカの独立にも主導的な役割を果たしました。独立戦争後もアメリカの多数派として、アメリカの文化や価値観の形成に最も強い影響力を持ち、政治的にも経済的にもアメリカでの主流派としての地位を確立していきました。

従って、後から上陸してきた移民たちは、当然ワスプの生活様式や価値観になじんでいくことがアメリカ人として認められていく第一歩となり、そうした影響は今でも色濃く残っています。1つの例をいえば、歴代の大統領のうち、1960年に就任したケネディ大統領（カトリック）以前は、全てがワスプの背景を持った人たちでした。

現在のアメリカは単にヨーロッパ系だけではなく、世界中から移民が押し寄せています。また、キリスト教系の移民を例にとっても、カトリック系の人々、たとえば、ラテン・アメリカの人々も多くアメリカに移住してきています。

Q ラテンアメリカ系（ヒスパニック系）の人々がアメリカにもたらした影響とはどのようなものですか？

ラテンアメリカ系の人々、すなわち中南米の人々はアメリカ合衆国の隣人として古くからアメリカに移住してきており、現在アメリカ国内のスペイン語を話す人口は5,000万人になろうとしています。そのうち、アメリカ人として帰化して、アメ

independence. After the War of Independence, WASPs exerted a strong influence in the formation of culture and values as the American majority. They eventually became the mainstream in the political and economic arenas.

As a consequence, the first step for later immigrants was to acclimatize themselves to the WASP lifestyle and values. This tendency is still obvious. All the American presidents before John F. Kennedy (inaugurated in 1960, and who was Catholic) had WASP backgrounds.

At present, immigrants come not only from Europe, but from all over the world. And Catholics form a good proportion of those immigrants who are Christian, for instance those arriving from Latin America.

Q What kind of influence have people from Latin countries had in the USA?

Latinos, that is to say people from Central and South America, have been immigrating to America since early times. The number of people in the States who speak Spanish is as high as 50 million. If we count the number of people who are already naturalized, some 40

リカに住んでいる人の数は、4,000万人近くになっているのです。

カリブや南米の人が多く暮らすニューヨークでは、地下鉄の中にもスペイン語の表示や広告がみられ、彼らのライフスタイルも食文化やアートと共にどんどん浸透してきています。そしてスペイン語は現在、アメリカで最も影響力のある外国語です。スペイン語を話す移民たちは、増え続けているのです。

Q　黒人とはどのような人たちのことですか？

現在4,045万人の黒人がアメリカ国内で生活しています。一口に黒人と言っても、そのルーツは様々です。黒人の祖先の多くはアフリカやカリブ海諸島から連れて来られた人々です。最近になってアフリカなどからやってきた人々もいます。また、黒人の中には、アメリカでの長い歴史のなかで、白人との間に生まれた人々やその子孫もかなりいます。

南部を中心に全米に拡散している黒人人口の多くは、その昔奴隷としてアフリカから強制的に連れて来られた人々です。奴隷制度は南部だけにあったのではなく、19世紀の初め頃までは、北部の州でも奴隷の売買が認められていました。アメリカに連れて来られた奴隷の総数は、1,000万人から

million Latinos live in the USA.

In New York, a city inhabited by many Caribbean and South American people, subway announcements and advertisements are often made in Spanish. Latino culture and lifestyle have penetrated deeply into America, with Latino food and art. Spanish is second only to English as the most widely spoken language in the States. The number of Spanish-speaking immigrants is only expected to keep growing.

Q Which people does the word "Blacks" refer to?

Currently, there are approximately 40.45 million black people in the USA. They have various roots. Many of their ancestors were originally brought from Africa or the Caribbean, but recently there has been a fresh wave of immigrants from Africa. Over the course of American history, the word "Black" also included mulattos or their children.

There are black populations dispersed all over the States, but particularly in the South. The majority are the descendants of Africans forced to come to the United States as slaves. It was not only in the South that the system of slavery existed: until the beginning of the nineteenth century, buying and selling slaves

1,200万人にものぼるというから驚かされます。しかし、劣悪な船旅と反乱などにより、最低に見積もっても200万人前後の人々がアメリカにやってくる途中、あるいはアメリカに上陸して間もなく死亡したといわれています。

『アンクル・トムの小屋』の1シーン。ストウ夫人(1811–96)の小説で、黒人奴隷のトムが非業の死を遂げる。南北戦争の一因になったとも言われる

　南部は南北戦争が終わるまで奴隷制度を採用していたため、現在でも黒人人口の多くは南部に集中しています。特にミシシッピ州では人口の37％、ルイジアナ州では32％が黒人系の人々です。しかも、こうした地域で黒人の人々が法的に全ての権利が保障され、平等に生活できるようになったのは、1964年に人種や性別などでの差別を禁止した公民権法が施行されてからのことでした。

　現在黒人系の人々は、アメリカで3番目に大きな人口を有するグループです。彼らの政治的なパワーは無視できず、人権問題や差別の問題などに取り組む核となる人々とみなされています。

Q 黒人系の人々のアメリカでの地位は、どのようになっているのですか？

　黒人の多くは奴隷の時代に始まって、長い間社会の底辺での生活を余儀なくされてきた人たちです。そうした経済的な問題は平等が保障された現在でも深刻で、貧しい黒人系の人々によって大都

was also permitted in the North. The total number of slaves brought to America is thought to have totaled 10 to 12 million—a startling figure. Due to poor traveling conditions at sea and to mutinies, at least 2 million people are estimated to have died, either on the way or upon arrival.

The South maintained the system of slavery until the end of the Civil War, which is why a large population of Blacks is still concentrated there. This is particularly true in the states of Mississippi, where 37% of the total population is Black, and Louisiana, where the number is 32%. It was only in 1964 that the rights of Black people came under equal protection by law. It was at this time that civil rights laws that prohibited discrimination by race or gender were passed.

At present, Blacks comprise the third largest ethnic group in America. Their political power cannot be ignored, and they are a core group in human rights and discrimination issues.

Q What is the social status of Blacks in the USA?

Since the period of slavery, large numbers of Black people have been forced to live at the lowest levels of society. Even after their equality had been guaranteed under law, they are still beset by serious economic

市が荒廃し、それが新たな偏見の原因となり、人種対立が深刻になるという悪循環が今のアメリカを悩ませています。

アメリカ史上初の黒人大統領、バラク・オバマ

ただ、黒人の人々の造り出した文化は、ジャズやブルースに代表されるように、今ではアメリカ文化を代表するものとして世界中に受け入れられています。アメリカ社会の中枢で活躍する黒人系の人々も目立ってきましたし、2008年にはバラク・オバマが初の黒人大統領となりました。黒人の人たちの高学歴者の比率も増えています。

なお、現在では黒人のことを、「ブラック」と呼ぶのではなく、「アフリカン・アメリカン」と表現します。黒人を差別していた時代に使われていた「ニグロ」という言葉も軽蔑的な表現とみなされています。

Q 「ユダヤ系のパワー」の真意は何ですか？

ユダヤ系の人々とは、特別な一つの人種を指すのではなく、ユダヤ教という宗教の元にまとまった人々のことで、アメリカでは、そうした人々の子孫をも含めてユダヤ系と表現しています。

ユダヤ系の人々は、ごく早い時期からアメリカの東海岸にやってきては交易などに従事していました。もともと、イギリスやオランダといった17世紀から18世紀のアメリカに影響力のあった国々が、産業を活性化する目的からもユダヤ人に対し

disadvantages. A vicious cycle is created, as poor Blacks live in inner-city slums and conditions deteriorate, giving rise to more prejudice and worse ethnic conflict.

Black culture can be credited with producing Jazz and Blues music, recognized worldwide and often taken as representing the culture of America. Numerous Black people have taken active roles in the center of American life—in 2008, Barack Obama became the first African American president of the United States. The percentage of Black people with high educational backgrounds is increasing.

These days, many people use the term "African American" instead of "Black." The word "Negro" is also considered pejorative since it was originally used when discrimination was the norm.

Q What is the real meaning of "Jewish Power"?

The term "Jewish" does not refer to any one specific ethnic group, but rather to all the peoples gathered under the religion of Judaism. In the USA, the term includes the descendants of these early immigrants.

Jews came to the East Coast very early on and engaged in commerce and trade. Countries like England and Holland, which had power and influence over America in the seventeenth and eighteenth centuries, had adopted open policies toward Jews in

ニューヨークにあるユダヤ系教会、シナゴーグ

て開放的な政策をとっていたために、早くから、多くのユダヤ系の金融資本がアメリカに流れてきたのです。

しかし、ユダヤ系の人々が本格的にアメリカに移住しだしたのは120年程前のことです。この時期、東欧やロシアからやってきた人々の多くは、故国での迫害を逃れて着のみ着のままでアメリカに渡り、アメリカでも貧困に耐えながら裁縫などの内職に従事していました。

しかし、ヨーロッパ各地で何世紀にも渡り、執拗に繰り返されてきたユダヤ人差別が、移民たちによってアメリカにも持ち込まれ、新大陸でも彼らは露骨な差別や迫害に直面することがありました。

従って、ユダヤ系の人々の多くは差別の少ない都市部にまとまりました。1930年代の統計によれば、ニューヨーク市の人口の25％がユダヤ系でした。そして法曹関係者だけをみると、その65％はユダヤ系の人々で占められていたといわれています。

また、同じ頃、ハリウッドの主要な映画産業の多くにも彼らはどんどん進出していきました。現在、ユダヤ系の背景をもつ人々はアメリカで最も成功した移民グループなのです。

Q なぜインディアンのことをネイティブ・アメリカンと呼ぶのですか？

以前は「インディアン」と呼ばれていたアメリ

order to promote business. A considerable amount of Jewish financial capital thus flowed into America from the early years.

Immigration of Jews into America on a large scale, however, only began about 120 years ago. This was a time when many Jews were fleeing persecution in Russia and Eastern Europe, and they arrived in America with only the clothes on their backs. They took up work in tailoring and other trades, enduring great poverty.

But discrimination against Jews, which had persisted for centuries in Europe, also found its way into America. Even in the New World, Jews became subject to discrimination and persecution.

Many Jewish people have therefore chosen to live all together in urban areas with less fear of persecution. In a 1930 census, 25% of the New York population, and 65% of those engaged in the legal profession, were said to be Jewish.

Jews also played a prominent part in the big movie industries in Hollywood. People of Jewish background are one of the most successful groups of immigrants in the USA.

Q Why are Indians called Native Americans?

The indigenous people of America were once called

カの先住民族のことを、現在では「ネイティブ・アメリカン」と呼ぶ習慣が定着しています。インディアンという言葉は、コロンブスがアメリカを発見したとき、そこをインドだと思っていたことに起因するもので、その後の白人系移民による先住民族の抑圧を象徴する言葉だという考え方があります。

ネイティブ・アメリカンという言葉は、彼らこそ、アメリカ大陸における先住民族だという意識を象徴しています。

特に、1960年代以降、ネイティブ・アメリカンの権利を主張する運動が展開され、それが実を結ぶ形で、従来のような差別や抑圧はほとんどなくなりました。この言葉はそうした運動の一環として彼らが勝ち得た表現なのです。

また、そうした動きを通して、ネイティブ・アメリカンの文化が広く紹介され、彼らの生活の知恵や思想がニューエイジの運動などにも大きな影響を与えました。しかし、長い間一般社会から疎外されてきた彼らを蝕む貧困の問題は、今でも深刻です。21世紀の中盤にはネイティブ・アメリカンの人口は540万人に達するだろうと予測されていますが、今後彼らが伝統を維持しながら、どのように生活レベルを向上していくか、課題の多いところです。

アメリカに住むネイティブ・アメリカンの一部族、ズニ族の女性

Indians, but now it is customary to refer to term as "Native Americans." The name "Indian" derives from Christopher Columbus's mistaken belief that he had discovered India when he came to America. To some, the name is an embodiment of white immigrant oppression of the indigenous people.

The term Native American is therefore symbolic of the awareness that these are the native peoples of America.

After the 1960s, a movement to assert the rights of Native Americans grew up, and it led to the abolishment of much long-standing discrimination and oppression. The word "Native American" is an expression of the success of this campaign.

Native American culture was widely publicized as a result, and their ways of thinking and practical wisdom exerted considerable influence over the New Age movement. Nevertheless, having existed on the edge of society for so many years, Native Americans are still beset by a serious problem of poverty. The Native American population is expected to reach 5.4 million by the mid twenty-first century. Improving their standard of living while maintaining their traditions remains their primary challenge.

Q ネイティブ・アメリカンと一般のアメリカ人との関係はどのように推移していったのですか？

　ネイティブ・アメリカンは、1万5,000年以上前にアジアから現在のベーリング海を経由してアメリカ大陸に移り住んだとされています。ヨーロッパの入植者が本格的に入り始めた16世紀には、現在のアメリカ合衆国に200万人程のネイティブ・アメリカンが居住していたのではないかと推定されています。ネイティブ・アメリカンは全米に拡散し、1,000を超える言語と様々な部族から構成されていました。

　ヨーロッパ系の人々が最初にアメリカに上陸してきたときは、彼らはおおむね友好的でした。しかし、その後入植者の持ち込んだ疫病で多くの部族が絶滅しました。白人の数が増えるにしたがって、敵対するケースも多くなり、特に18世紀にフランスとイギリスが新大陸での主導権争いをしたとき、ネイティブ・アメリカンも戦争に巻き込まれました。その折にイギリス軍が天然痘の細菌のついた毛布をネイティブ・アメリカンに配ったこともありました。

　19世紀になって、西部への開拓が進むにつれ、さらにネイティブ・アメリカンの人々が厳しい立場に追い込まれたことは周知の事実です。この結果、19世紀末には、ネイティブ・アメリカンの人口は24万人前後にまで激減したのです。

ネイティブ・アメリカンを駆逐する白人を描いた絵

Q How have relations between Native Americans and other Americans changed?

It is said that Native Americans immigrated to America more than 15,000 years ago, across the Bering Sea from Asia. It is estimated that about 2 million Native Americans inhabited the USA in the sixteenth century, when the first European settlers arrived on a large scale. There were Native Americans all over the USA in various tribes speaking more than 1,000 languages.

Native Americans were generally quite welcoming when the first Europeans arrived. However, many native tribes died from epidemics brought by the settlers. Confrontation increased as the number of Whites increased. Native Americans found themselves embroiled in the eighteenth-century struggle between French and English sovereignty in the New World. The British Army even distributed blankets infected with smallpox germs to Native Americans.

As is well known, Native Americans were pushed into desperate circumstances as the Western Frontier moved ever westward in the course of the nineteenth century. By the end of the century the Native American population had declined sharply, to around 240,000.

Q 一般のアメリカ人はネイティブ・アメリカンからどのような影響を受けたのですか？

アメリカにきたヨーロッパ系の人々は、最初の頃からネイティブ・アメリカンの風習やコミュニケーションのスタイルを自らの生活の中に取り入れていきました。

イロコイ族の交易の様子。民主主義政治のヒントになったとも言われる

特に東北部に拡散していたイロコイ族が行っていた部族会議が大変民主的であったことから、独立戦争の頃に、アメリカの指導者たちがイロコイ族の手法をアメリカ流の民主主義政治のヒントにしたという話も残っています。また、アメリカ人の相手の目をしっかりと見つめながら、大きな声で自己を主張する風習もネイティブ・アメリカンとの交流の中で培われたものといわれています。

また、20世紀になって、ネイティブ・アメリカンの素朴な生活が紹介されるにつれ、彼らの芸術や工芸、あるいは儀式や伝統がアメリカの芸術に大きな影響を与えたのもまた事実です。

Q ダイバーシティとはどういうことを指すのですか？

ダイバーシティとは「多様性」という意味の英語です。そして、これは大変積極的な意味をもった言葉です。

様々な移民が集まり国を造っているアメリカは、まさに多様性の国といえましょう。多様な人々が

Q   What influences did Americans receive from Native Americans?

European immigrants adopted some of the customs and communication methods of Native Americans from early times.

One such custom was the tribal meeting, originally conducted by the Iroquois tribe, who lived all over the Northeast. It is said that at the time of the Civil War American leaders used ideas from the Iroquois system in drawing up the kind of democratic government they themselves wanted. The American way of looking one's speaking partner straight in the eye and asserting oneself in a loud voice is also said to have been fostered during exchanges with Native Americans.

It is also a fact that in the twentieth century, as the simple lifestyle of Native Americans became more widely known, their arts, crafts, rituals, and traditions exerted a tremendous influence on American art.

Q   What does the word "diversity" mean?

Diversity is an English word meaning "variety," and it has very positive nuances.

America is a country composed of various groups of immigrants. It is, literally, a country of diversity.

多彩なアイデアを出し合い、競っていくことが、アメリカという国のエネルギー源となっています。

従って、民族の数がますます増え、共存している現在では、「ダイバーシティ」こそ、アメリカにとって最も大切な価値観ということになったのです。

ところで、「ダイバーシティ」とは、「メルティング・ポット（人種のるつぼ）」、または「サラダ・ボウル社会」をさらに発展的に解釈し、積極的に捉えていった言葉で、皆がそれぞれの民族性を維持しながら、アメリカ人としてアメリカという国家を拠り所に生きていこうという意味なのです。

前のニューヨーク市長ディンキンズ氏が、ダイバーシティを評して「美しきモザイク」と言ったことが話題になりました。このコメントの通り、ダイバーシティは、多彩な人種や文化背景をもつ人が集まるアメリカ社会への強いアピールをもった言葉なのです。

Q アメリカでは英語が「国語」なのですか？

実はアメリカ合衆国には英語が国語であるということを規定した法律はないのです。また、現在アメリカには英語を母国語としない人、すなわち英語を第2外国語として生活している人が約5,500万人もいます。これはアメリカ全人口の20％弱に相当し、こうした人々は特に都市部に集中してい

Its people present a variety of competing ideas, which provide the country's source of energy.

Nowadays, there is an extraordinary number of different ethnic groups in the USA, and they must all co-exist. "Diversity" has become one of the most important values in America.

"Diversity" is an extension of the phrase "melting pot" or "salad bowl society" with the positive nuances stressed. It refers to the fact that people can make the USA their own country, even while they maintain their ethnic identities.

The former mayor of New York, David Dinkins, once made a famous comment; he described diversity as a "beautiful mosaic." As the phrase indicates, diversity is a word that has strong appeal for American society, a nation composed of many different people, with various racial and cultural backgrounds.

Q   Is English the national language in the USA?

There is in fact no law stipulating that English is the national language of the USA. There are as many as 55 million Americans whose mother tongue is another language altogether, and who speak English as a second language. They amount to 20% of the total population, and are concentrated in urban areas. In recent decades

ます。最近では、こうした傾向を心配した人たちによる、英語を国語にしようという動きもあるのです。

　また、カリフォルニアの小学校では、中米からの子供が多くなったことから、英語ではなくスペイン語での授業を実施している学校もあります。そこでは、もともと英語を話す子供もスペイン語を習い、スペイン語を母国語として話す子供との交流を促進しているのです。

　ただ、東西両海岸の都市部を別として、さらにメキシコ系の人々の多い南西部を除けば、アメリカは英語社会です。こうしたことも、都市と地方との生活環境の違いを示す大きな要因となっているようです。

アメリカの地域性

Q　ニューイングランドとはどんな地域ですか？

　ニューイングランドはアメリカの東北部、マサチューセッツ、メイン、バーモント、ニューハンプシャー、ロードアイランド、コネチカットの６州で構成されています。最大の都市はボストンで、

there has been an effort by some, concerned by this trend, to propose that English become the national language.

In some Californian elementary schools, the number of Central American children has increased so much that classes are offered in Spanish rather than English. English-speaking children learn Spanish to have more chance of making friends with Spanish-speaking children.

But apart from urban areas on the East and West Coasts, and if one excepts the Southwest with its large population of Mexican-Americans, most of the country is English-speaking. This is a large factor in the difference between urban provincial areas as living environments.

The Differences in Regions in the USA

Q What kind of region is New England?

New England is a region in the northeast of the USA consisting of six states: Massachusetts, Maine, Vermont, New Hampshire, Rhode Island, and Connecticut. The largest city is Boston, with a population of 667,000

人口は約66.7万人(全米23位)。ニューイングランド地域の総人口は1,473万人となります。

ニューイングランドの起こりは、バージニアの植民地を開いたことでも知られる探検家、ジョン・スミスが1614年にこの地を探検し、ニューイングランドと命名したことによります。その後、あのメイフラワー号で大西洋を渡ってきたピルグリム・ファーザーズの一行が、現在のマサチューセッツ州のプリマスに移住して以来、ニューイングランドは、北アメリカで最も古い入植地の1つとして、開墾されていきました。

1910年ごろのプリマスの風景

それは、ピルグリム・ファーザーズの半数が最初の冬を越せなかったといわれるくらい、過酷な環境の中での開拓事業でした。

ニューイングランド気質といえば、勤勉で教育熱心、公共への福祉を重んじ、ボランティア精神が旺盛といった、古くからの、特にピルグリム・ファーザーズ以来のプロテスタントの伝統を受け継いだものといえます。マサチューセッツ州が自州のコマーシャルの中で、「マサチューセッツの心はアメリカの心」というコピーを使っているのは、こうした伝統的な地域性をPRしたものに他なりません。

(23rd in the USA). The total population of New England is 14,730,000.

New England was so named by John Smith, the famous explorer who founded the Virginia colony. He explored the area in 1614. Later, when the Pilgrims came across the Atlantic in the Mayflower, they moved into Plymouth, Massachusetts. It was then that New England began to develop. It is one of the oldest colonies in North America.

The Pilgrims tried to create colonies in a very harsh environment, and half of the first settlers did not survive the first winter.

The spirit of New England consists of diligence, enthusiasm for education, respect for public welfare, and active volunteering, all of which derive from the old Protestant tradition of the Pilgrims. In its promotional material the state of Massachusetts states that "the heart of Massachusetts is the heart of America," emphasizing the traditionalism of the region.

Q ニューヨークとロサンゼルスは東西の文化を代表しているのですか？

東の文化を代表するブロードウェイ

西の文化を代表するハリウッド

東部最大の産業都市ニューヨークと、カリフォルニア州最大の都市圏を構成しているロサンゼルスとは、まさに東海岸と西海岸の特徴を代表したライバルであるといえましょう。

まず、何といってもニューヨークは古い歴史があり、伝統のある街です。それに対してロサンゼルス地区は20世紀になって急成長を遂げた広大な都市空間です。

例えば、ニューヨークを代表するショービジネスがブロードウェイ・ミュージカルなら、ロサンゼルスには巨大なセットとロケで造り上げられるハリウッド映画があります。

地下鉄と徒歩で目的地に行くのがニューヨーカーなら、フリーウェイからパームツリーの下にある駐車場に車を停め、メキシコ風のカラフルなオフィスを訪ねるのがロサンゼルスの人たちの毎日です。

冬にニューヨークから飛行機に乗るときはコートにマフラーのいでたちで、ロサンゼルスの空港に到着すれば、シャツ１枚でもOKというぐらい気候も違います。

さらに、町で活躍する人々を見渡せば、ニューヨークにはヨーロッパ各地からの多様な移民にカリブからの人々、アジアの移民が目立っています。

Q Do New York and Los Angeles represent East and West Coast cultures?

New York, the largest industrial city in the East, and Los Angeles, the largest urban area in California, each represent East Coast and West Coast characteristics, and they are rather like rivals.

New York is a city that has an old history and tradition, while Los Angeles is a huge urban area that developed rapidly during the twentieth century.

For example, whereas show business in New York consists of Broadway musicals, Los Angeles has Hollywood movies made with gigantic sets and studio locations.

New Yorkers travel by subway and on foot, while Los Angeleans drive the freeways, park their cars in lots under palm trees, and go to their offices in colorful Mexican-style buildings.

The climates differ greatly as well. One needs a coat and muffler when boarding a plane in the New York winter, but arriving at LAX airport during the same season, all one needs is a shirt.

In New York, one can see many immigrants from Europe, the Caribbean, and Asia in the working population in the city. In LA one sees various Asians

ロサンゼルスは、アジア各国の人の他に、ラテン・アメリカ、とくにメキシコの移住者が膨大な量流れ込んでいます。

このように、イーストコーストとウエストコーストとは、地理的にアメリカの両海岸に分かれているというだけでなく、異なった地域性を誇っているのです。

Q ミッドウエスト（ハートランド）とはどのような地域ですか？

アメリカのど真ん中にあたる地域のことをハートランドと呼びます。アパラチア山脈を越えれば、そこから先は平原がはるかロッキー山脈まで続いています。南部を除いたこの広い地域を、ミッドウエスト（中西部）と人は呼びますが、このミッドウエストのニックネームがハートランドなのです。ミッドウエストのど真ん中を扇のように無数の支流が拡散するミシシッピ川が流れています。

とうもろこしや小麦、そして酪農のさかんなこの地域はほとんどが農地です。道はどこまでも一直線で、山はどこにもありません。緑は豊かで、冬は厳しく、夏は結構暑く、雷を伴った激しい豪雨が襲ってくることもあれば、竜巻だって起こります。

中西部の農場風景 by Dabid Ball

ハートランドに住む人々は、この広い大地を開

and a lot of Latin Americans, particularly immigrants from Mexico.

Thus, not only are the East and West Coasts geographically separate, they also have very different regional characteristics.

Q What is the Midwest, or the "Heartland," like as a region?

The region right at the center of the USA is called the Heartland. It is a vast plain beyond the Appalachian Mountains that extends all the way to the Rockies. People call this vast region the Midwest (though this does not cover the South), but its nickname is the Heartland. The Mississippi and its numerous tributaries spread out over the Heartland like a fan.

This region is predominantly farmland: there is a lot of corn, wheat, and dairy farming. Roads go straight on, seemingly without end, without a mountain or hill in sight. The area is noted for its rich greenery, harsh winters, and hot summers, as well as torrential thunderstorms. Tornadoes also hit the region from time to time.

The inhabitants of the Heartland are descendants of

拓し農耕を営んできた人々の子孫で、特にプロテスタントを信仰するヨーロッパ系の人々が多く、今でも質素で保守的な生活を維持している人々が多くいます。

Q サウス（南部）とはどのような地域ですか？

ワシントンD.C.からポトマック川を渡れば、そこはもうバージニア州。バージニア州はすでにサウスの一部となります。南部といえば、「風と共に去りぬ」の映画をイメージする人も多いでしょう。

南部はアメリカでも最も古くから開拓されてきた地域です。しかし、アメリカが独立してしばらく経つと、南部の経済は北部で発達した工業や金融業の影響を強く受けるようになります。そうした北部の経済支配への反発こそが、あの南北戦争の原因となったわけです。

南軍の指揮官リー将軍

北部と戦った南部には、今でも南部としての強いプライドが残っています。南部の中心都市ともいえるジョージア州のアトランタには、南北戦争当時の南軍の総指揮官リー将軍の銅像が今も堂々とした姿を披露しています。

成長を続けるアトランタの金融街

南北戦争の後、長い間、南部は経済的にも立ち後れ、奴隷解放後も人種差別が残るなど、暗いイメージがつきまといました。

the people who cultivated this vast land and developed its agriculture—mostly European Protestant immigrants. Many of them have simple and conservative lifestyles.

Q What kind of region is the South?

Crossing the Potomac river from Washington, D.C., one arrives in the state of Virginia. Virginia is a part of the South, a region that, no doubt, many people associate with the movie "Gone with the Wind."

The South was one of the first regions to be colonized. Soon after Independence, however, the Southern economy was greatly affected by industry and financial developments in the North. Opposition against the economic control of the North led to the Civil War.

A strong Southern pride is still evident in the South. This pride is related to the struggle against the North. In Atlanta, Georgia, one can see the imposing bronze statue of General Lee, the Commander-in-Chief of the Confederate Army.

After the Civil War, a dark image haunted the South. It was seen as lagging behind the North economically, and as a place where racial discrimination still existed long after slaves were liberated.

独特ななまりのある英語と、温暖な気候と風土。
「サザン・ホスピタリティ」と呼ばれる親切な気質、
そしてケージャンなどに代表される南部独特の料
理など、南部の旅の魅力を語ればきりがありませ
ん。

南部の総人口は約1億900万人。最も人口の多い
州は、フロリダ（約1,850万人）です。南部はアメリ
カの中の有望株の1つで、アメリカ経済を牽引し
ていく重要な役割も担っているのです。

Southerners speak English with striking accents, and the Southern weather and climate is mild. These elements, coupled with a kind temperament, referred to as "Southern Hospitality," as well as delicious regional dishes such as Cajun cooking, all contribute to its appeal for tourists.

The South's total population is 109 million. The largest population is in Florida (18.5 million). The South is one of the most promising regions in the USA and is expected to continue to play an important role in the American economy.

◆コラム◆ アメリカの地域性と大統領選挙

　アメリカは東西両海岸に国際的な都市が多くあります。例えば東海岸でいえばニューヨークやボストン。西海岸でいえばシアトル、サンフランシスコ、そしてロサンゼルス。

　そこは昔から海外からの移民の玄関口でもありました。ですから、この地域はどちらかというと移民の権利や多様性を許容しようという意識に敏感な地域なのです。

　さらにこれらの地域には、アメリカの経済を牽引し、シアトル郊外にあるマイクロソフトのような世界の最先端をいく国際企業も多く活動しています。

　政治的にいえば、東西両海岸の都市部こそが、リベラル派の票田となるのです。直近の大統領選挙でいうなら、民主党のヒラリー・クリントン候補への支持票が集中したのもこの地域です。

　逆に、アメリカ中部は保守的で伝統を重んずる人々が多く住みます。アメリカの穀倉地帯であり、古くからプロテスタント系の人々が多く住むこの地域は、勤勉実直で、宗教的にもプロテスタントの伝統を守ろうとする人が多く住みます。特にアメリカ中西部と呼ばれる地域は、バイブル・ベルト地帯と呼ばれるように、日曜日は教会に集い、家族と地域のコミュニティを大切にする人々が集まっているのが特徴です。

　変化するアメリカに警鐘を鳴らそうとしたドナルド・トランプ候補を支持した多くの人は、この地域に住む人々でした。

　このように、アメリカは海岸部と中央部とでは人の考え方、ライフスタイルにも大きな違いが見受けられるのです。

Chapter 2

History and Background of the USA

第2章 アメリカの歴史と背景

アメリカの国歌と国旗

Q アメリカの国歌では何が歌われているのですか？

「星条旗よ永遠なれ」が、正式に国歌として採用されたのは、1931年3月のことですが、実はこの歌は19世紀前半につくられたものです。1812年、ヨーロッパでのナポレオン戦争が飛び火する形で、アメリカはイギリスと開戦しました。戦いは14年まで続き、アメリカは苦戦します。一時はワシントンD.C.までイギリス軍が侵攻する騒ぎまで起きたほどです。

詩人フランシス・スコット・キー(1779–1843)。The Star-Spangled Banner の歌詞を書いた

この戦争の最中、イギリスの軍艦に監禁されていたアメリカ人の法律家フランシス・スコット・キーが、イギリス海軍の砲火にもめげず煙のむこうに立っていた星条旗を夜明けに船から観て感動して作ったのが、「星条旗よ永遠なれ」の愛国詩だったのです。

この詩はたちまちアメリカに流行しましたが、その詩についた音楽は、当時イギリスの居酒屋などで流行っていた「天国のアナクレオンへ」という飲み歌のメロディでした。

このメロディの作曲家は、ちなみにジョン・スタフォード・スミスというイギリス人。対戦相手であるイギリス人のメロディを拝借して愛国歌を

National Anthem and Flag

Q What is the national anthem of the USA?

"The Star-Spangled Banner" was officially adopted as the national anthem in March 1931, but the song actually dates from the early nineteenth century. The Napoleonic Wars in Europe provided the spark that caused America to open hostilities against England in 1812. The war continued until 1814, and it was a tough battle for America. British troops even got as far as invading Washington, D.C. at one time during the conflict.

The words to "The Star-Spangled Banner" come from a patriotic poem composed by the American lawyer Francis Scott Key. Confined in a British warship, he was moved to write the poem when he caught sight of a Star-Spangled banner still fluttering beyond the smoke, undaunted by the British gunfire.

The poem soon became very popular in the USA, but the tune actually came from a British song, "To Anacreon in Heaven," popularly sung in English taverns.

The composer was a British named John Stafford Smith. It is amusing to think that what became the American national anthem borrowed its original tune

つくり、それがアメリカ中に広まったという不思議な歌が、現在のアメリカの国歌なのです。

Q アメリカの国旗はどのようにしてデザインされたのですか？

1795年ごろの星条旗。星の数から15州であることがわかる

現在の星条旗

アメリカの国旗は星が州の数を、赤と青の縞模様が独立当時の13州を表しているということは周知の事実でしょう。

独立当初は、デザインに決まりがあったわけではなく、とりあえず星は円形に配列するのが習わしでした。しかし、それとてもはっきりとした規準はなく、様々なデザインの旗が作られ、公式行事などで利用されていたのです。

最初はそれでよかったのですが、その後、1791年にバーモント州が、そしてその翌年にはケンタッキー州が新たな州として加わることになりました。そこで、星の数もストライプの数もそれぞれ15にしたのですが、その後も続々と合衆国に編入される州が増えたため、1818年の議会で、今後は13州のみを縞模様で示し、州の数を星で示すことが正式に決定されたのです。

アメリカの旗には、独立後に1州、また1州と増えていき、アメリカという国家の体裁をじょじょに整えていった事実を象徴するような話があるのです。アメリカの国旗が現在のようになったのは1959年にハワイが50番目の州となったときです。

from a country against whom it had fought a war.

Q What is the history of the design of American flag?

As everybody knows, the American flag is composed of stars, which indicate the number of states. The red and blue stripes represent the thirteen states at the time of Independence.

During colonial times, no specific format for a flag existed other than that the stars were usually arranged in a circle. Since there was no set standard, freely designed flags were used for public events.

At first this was quite satisfactory. Then, Vermont and Kentucky joined the Confederation in 1791 and 1792 respectively, and the number of stars and stripes increased to fifteen. As still more states joined, Congress decided in 1818 that only the first thirteen states would be shown as stripes, and the total number of states would be shown as stars.

The American flag is a symbol of the process the USA underwent in the course of its construction as a nation; state after state was added once Independence had been gained. The current flag with fifty stars was designed in 1959 when Hawaii became the fiftieth state in the USA.

アメリカの歴史

Q アメリカはどれくらい古い国なのですか？

アメリカが国家としてイギリスからの独立を宣言したのは1776年のことですから、国家として成立してから、240年少々しか経過していないことになります。ただし、正式に独立国家として諸外国に承認されたのは1783年のことですから、その時点から独立国となったとするなら、アメリカはさらに若い国になります。

そして、この若さこそが、旧来の風習や伝統に束縛されずに国家がのびのびと発展し、短期間で世界をリードする大国となった理由の1つなのです。

北アメリカに最初に住んだ人々

アジア系の人々が凍結したベーリング海を渡って、シベリアからアラスカに入り、南北アメリカに散っていったのが、3万年から1万年前とされる

ただし、北米（大陸）には、アメリカが国家として独立するずっと以前から、ネイティブ・アメリカンによる無数の部族国家があったことも忘れてはならない事実です。彼らがアメリカに住み着いたのは、2万年以上の昔と推定されますから、こうした事実を加味すると、アメリカにも相当古くから国家の起源となる文化があったことになります。

The History of the USA

Q How old is America?

America declared independence from England in 1776, so it has been only about 240 years since America was founded as a nation. Official acknowledgment as an independent country by other countries, however, was not made until 1783. If one counts that date as its inception, the USA is even younger as a country.

This relative youth is one reason why the USA developed quickly to become a world power in a short period of time. It was unrestricted by old customs or traditions.

However, one should not forget a nation consisting of numerous tribes of Native Americans existed in North America from well before Independence. It was approximately 20,000 years ago that Native Americans first settled in the States. If one takes this fact into consideration, a much older culture existed in America that provided the starting point for the nation.

Q アメリカは独立する前はどのような状態だったのですか？

　ネイティブ・アメリカンの土地であったアメリカがヨーロッパに紹介されたのは、15世紀末頃のことです。有名なコロンブスの西インド諸島への航海が1492年。その後16世紀には数多くの探検家が北アメリカに上陸し、スペインやイギリス、そしてオランダなどに新大陸の情報を紹介しました。

　その後、本格的に入植がはじまったのは、17世紀前半のことです。東部海岸には主にイギリスやオランダからの入植者が、南部や現在のテキサスにはスペインの人々が、そしてメキシコ湾から内陸部にかけては、フランス人が上陸しました。

1650年代のニュー・アムステルダムの風景

　入植者の多くはヨーロッパで宗教的な迫害を受けた人々や、ヨーロッパの列強から組織的に送り込まれた人々でした。ニューヨークを例にとれば、16世紀の前半にオランダ人がマンハッタン島の南端にニュー・アムステルダムという植民地を開いたのがその起こりです。1650年代のニュー・アムステルダムには、1,500人の人々が生活し、15の言語が話されていたといいます。

　独立戦争の前までに、アメリカは東部や南部を中心にヨーロッパからの背景をもった多様な入植者が続々と上陸し、開墾し、村を造り、独自の決まりに従って、それぞれの植民地を運営していました。

　彼らは、新大陸という広大な土地に散らばって、

Q What was America like before Independence?

It was at the end of the fifteenth century that Europeans first gained access to America, the land of the Native Americans. Columbus made his famous voyage to the West Indies in 1492. Later, in the sixteenth century, numerous explorers landed in North America and introduced the New Continent to Spain, England, and Holland.

Full-scale settlement started in the early seventeenth century. British and Dutch settled mostly in the East Coast; Spanish settled in the South and also in present-day Texas; French settled in an area stretching from the Gulf of Mexico further inland.

Many of the settlers were fleeing religious persecution in Europe, or had been officially sent by the major European powers. For example, New York originated when the Dutch opened a colony called New Amsterdam in lower Manhattan in the early sixteenth century. In 1650s, 1,500 people lived in New Amsterdam, speaking fifteen different languages.

Various groups of Europeans with diverse backgrounds had thus come to the East and the South to settle before the War of Independence. They developed the land, creating villages and running colonies in their own styles.

The settlers lived in clusters all over the vast

集団で生活し、それぞれが自らの故国、あるいは宗主国であるイギリスに忠誠を誓いながらも、植民地として統一された社会を望んでいたわけではなく、そうした意識もありませんでした。

こうした独立当時のアメリカの伝統が受け継がれ、小さな中央政府のもと、地方が独自に法律や制度を定めていこうというアメリカ人の意識の源流となっていったのです。

Q　どのような経緯でアメリカは独立の道を選んだのですか？

独立戦争の導火線になったのは、北アメリカの領有権を巡ってイギリスとフランスとが、ネイティブ・アメリカンを交えて戦ったフレンチ・インディアン戦争（1755–1763）にあります。戦争は、イギリスの勝利に終わりますが、この戦争でかかった費用をイギリス本国が増税の形で植民地の人たちに押しつけようとしたことと、イギリスが植民地の人々のアパラチア山脈より西側への移動を禁止して、この広大な地域をイギリスが直接支配しようとしたことが植民地の人々の反発を招き、独立戦争へと繋がっていったのです。

特に、アメリカに対するイギリス本国の一方的な課税に対して、アメリカ側はイギリスの議会に代表を送っていないのに課税するのは植民地の権利を踏みにじるものとして抗議し、ボストン茶会

continent. Though they pledged loyalty to their mother country or their sovereign state of England, they did not hope to be a unified colony, nor were they even aware of themselves as such.

This early tradition of independence became the origin of the common American view, which holds true even today, that regional governments should establish their own laws and institutions, and central government should be limited.

Q How did America decide to become independent?

The War of Independence had its origins in the French and Indian Wars fought between England and France over control of North American territories—wars in which Native Americans too were involved. England won, but the British government then tried to recoup war expenses by raising settlers' taxes. In an effort to assert its authority, Britain also prohibited settlers from moving beyond the Appalachian Mountains. The settlers rebelled, and this led to the War of Independence.

The settlers were particularly upset by England's unilateral tax imposition, which they viewed as an abuse of the rights of a colony since it had no representation in the British Parliament. Demonstrations grew

紅茶箱を海に投げるボストン茶会事件の様子

事件として知られるボストンでの抗議行動は激化し、緊張が高まりました。これに対して、イギリス側が植民地の人々の武器を奪い、武力で対抗しようとしたことが、独立戦争への直接の引き金になったのです。

Q 独立戦争はどのように推移したのですか？

独立戦争の初めの頃は、イギリスの精鋭部隊に対して、植民地側のにわか作りの部隊は連戦連敗でした。しかも、全ての人々が独立を願ったわけではなく、多くの人はいまだにイギリスへの忠誠心を捨てきれないでいたのも事実でした。

しかし、イギリス軍は植民地の親英派の人々をうまく活用できず、外交上もイギリスのライバルであったフランスが植民地軍にテコ入れをして参戦するなどというミスが続き、だんだんと形成が不利になっていきました。独立革命軍はジョージ・ワシントンの指導力の元、勢力を挽回し、ついにパリでの講和条約でアメリカの13州は独立国家として認められるに至ったのです。

アメリカ初代大統領、ジョージ・ワシントン

particularly intense in Boston, known for its "Boston Tea Party," and tension rose. England counteracted by force, depriving the settlers of weapons. This was the direct cause of the war.

Q What were the various stages in the War of Independence (The American Revolution)?

At the start of the war, the colonial troops, which had been hastily prepared, suffered one defeat after another at the hands of British troops. Not all of the settlers desired independence, and many of them found it difficult to discard their loyalty to England.

England, however, found it difficult to make the best use of pro-British settlers in the colonies. It also failed on a diplomatic level—its rival France ended up supporting the colonies and participating in the war. England began suffering defeats and the tables turned. The Revolutionary Army, led by George Washington, gained its full power, and the thirteen states of America were finally acknowledged as an independent nation at the Peace Conference in Paris.

Q 独立した後のアメリカはどのような状態だったのですか？

パリ条約
アメリカが独立革命を締結させた条約。イギリスはアメリカの独立を承認した。

1783年に結ばれたパリ条約でアメリカが独立国として獲得したのは、ミシシッピ川以東の領土でした。一応独立は達成しましたが、もともと単なる寄り合い所帯だったアメリカでは、この時点から国をどのように造っていくか話し合わなければなりませんでした。

問題は、強い政府を嫌い、自由を求めて立ち上がった植民地の人々の意見をどうまとめ、新しい中央政府を作るかということでした。多くの人が自分の町や村は自分たちで管理したいと思い、強い中央政府を造ることに疑問を抱いていたのです。

その後も地方の自治を尊重すべきという人と、統一国家としての秩序を重んずる人との間の政治的対立はしばらく続き、1801年に3代目の大統領に就いたジェファーソンは、前者の立場をとる政党リパブリカンズの代表として、アレクサンダー・ハミルトンが率いる、強い政府を求める人々の結成したフェデラリストという政党と激しく対立しました。

この強い政府を主張する考え方は、現在の民主党に、個人と地方の自治を強調する人々は現在の共和党に今なお影響を与え、アメリカの世論を常に2つに分けています。レーガン大統領の唱えた小さい政府、それに対してクリントン大統領のいう国民健康保険構想などに代表される中央政府の

Q What situation did America find itself in after independence?

America finally obtained its independence at the 1783 Treaty of Paris, obtaining all the territory east of the Mississippi. But much discussion still remained on how the country, previously just a loose conglomeration of people, was to build itself into a nation.

The problem was persuading the colonists, who had fought hard for their freedom and abhorred strong government, of the need to establish a new central government. Many people wanted to manage their own towns or villages, and held suspicions about a strong central government.

Confrontation continued for a while between those who held regional autonomy in high regard, and those who supported the Confederation. In 1801 the confrontation intensified when the third President, Thomas Jefferson, a Republican, supported regional autonomy, while the Federalists, led by Alexander Hamilton, supported the Confederation.

Support for strong government is still reflected in the views of contemporary Democrats. The assertion of the rights of the individual and the autonomy of local governments is reflected in the modern Republican Party. American public opinion is divided in this way all the time. The small government advocated by

権限強化は、元をたどれば独立戦争の頃からの論争に起因しているのです。

Q いつ頃アメリカは西に向かって発展し始めたのですか？

ルイジアナ買収の対象地域
（太枠内）

独立戦争の頃から19世紀初頭にかけて、西部といえばアメリカ東部を南北に走るアパラチア山脈以西のことを指していました。

このアパラチア山脈以西の広大な土地を最初に探検したのはスペイン人でした。しかし、その後、17世紀にはフランス人がこの流域に入植し、開墾事業に従事します。彼らは、フランスのルイ王朝の土地という意味のルイジアナ植民地をそこに開きます。それはミシシッピ川流域に沿って南はニューオリンズから北はカナダとの国境、そして西はロッキー山脈にいたる広大な地域でした。それをアメリカがヨーロッパでの戦争で戦費の調達に苦しむナポレオンから破格の値段で購入したのが1803年のことでした。この「ルイジアナ・パーチェス」によって、アメリカはいよいよ西に向かって発展をはじめたのです。

former president Ronald Reagan and the strengthening of the role of central government as represented by former president Clinton's Health and Social Welfare Plan can both be traced back to arguments originating at the time of Independence.

Q When did westward development start in America?

During the period from the War of Independence to the beginning of the nineteenth century, the word "West" meant west of the Appalachian Mountains, which run south to north in the East.

It was the Spanish who first explored the vast lands to the west of these Appalachian Mountains. Later, in the seventeenth century, the French colonized and cultivated the area. They opened a colony called Louisiana, or "the land of the Louis Dynasty." This vast land extended south to New Orleans and north to the Canadian border along the Mississippi River, and west to the Rockies. America purchased it at an extremely good price in 1803 from Napoleon, who badly needed to raise money for his war in Europe. With the Louisiana Purchase, westward development could begin at last.

特に1830年代頃から西海岸の肥沃な土地を求めて膨大な数の開拓者が西へと移動をはじめ、それに伴ってフロンティアと呼ばれる辺境地も西へと位置を変えていきました。

　1849年以降のゴールドラッシュなどによって比較的早い時期に開発の進んだ西海岸と、東からの入植者によってじわりじわりと西へ押されていったフロンティアとの境界線が消滅したのは1890年頃のことといわれています。

Q　テキサス州はいつごろアメリカの一部になったのですか？

　テキサスは1836年にメキシコから独立した国家でした。もともとメキシコ領だったテキサスにアメリカ南東部から入植者が入り込み、綿花などの栽培をはじめたのは1820年代のことで、その人口は1830年代までに2万2,000人（内2,000人は奴隷）にもなりました。彼らはプロテスタントで、そのことがスペインの伝統をもち、カトリックを信仰するメキシコ人たちにとっておもしろくありません。しかも、当時テキサスには1,000人のメキシコ人しかいませんでした。

　そこでメキシコはアメリカ人の入植を禁止する措置に出たのです。それに反抗したアメリカ人入植者が1835年に独立のために立ち上がりました。この戦争で特に有名な出来事が、サンアントニオにあるアラモという僧院に立

1854年ごろのアラモの様子

Around 1830, a huge number of pioneers moved westward looking for fertile land, and the frontier moved westward accordingly.

The boundary between the West Coast, which had started being developed from 1849 with the Gold Rush, and the frontier, which the settlers from the East had been gradually pushing westward, finally disappeared around 1890.

Q When was Texas incorporated into the USA?

Texas gained independence from Mexico in 1836. American settlers from the southeast had already moved into Texas and established cotton plantations from around 1820. Their number had increased to 22,000 (2,000 of which were slaves) by 1830. These people were Protestants and unwelcome to the Mexicans who were Catholic and had Spanish traditions. There were only about 1,000 Mexicans in the area, and they felt severely outnumbered.

Mexico soon took measures to prohibit American settlement, so American settlers rose up against Mexico to fight for independence in 1835. The most famous event during the ensuing war was the fight to the death by men who had been holed up in a mission called the

てこもった独立を目指す人々が全員降伏を拒否して戦い、玉砕した事件でした。彼らは「アラモを忘れるな」のスローガンと共に、後世に語り伝えられ、ジョン・ウエインが主演した映画なども制作されています。

その後、メキシコ軍を打ち破り独立したテキサスが、アメリカ合衆国に加わったのは1845年のことでした。テキサスの大都会ヒューストンは、軍を率いた英雄サム・ヒューストンの名前をとったものです。

Q オレゴン・トレイルとはどのようなイベントだったのですか？

1830年代から1860年代にかけて、当時のアメリカの総人口の50人に1人が、このトレイルという道なき道を通って、現在のオレゴン州ポートランドへと旅立ちました。当時オレゴンには肥沃な農地があって、そこを開拓した人にはその土地が無償で与えられたのです。東部での貧しい暮らしを捨て、あるいはさらに豊かになるチャンスを求めて、数えきれない人々がカンザスシティの東にあるインディペンデンスという街に集まってきました。当時そこまでは船などを乗り継いで東海岸からやってこれたのです。

インディペンデン

遥か未開の地を進むオレゴン・トレイル

Alamo in San Antonio. The story of this incident has been handed down from generation to generation, along with the slogan "Remember the Alamo." A famous movie starring John Wayne was made about this incident.

In 1845, Texas defeated Mexico, won its independence, and was incorporated into the USA. Houston was named after Sam Houston, one of the heroes who led the war.

Q What was the Oregon Trail?

From 1830 to 1860, one out of fifty Americans embarked on a journey along an unmarked trail toward Portland, Oregon. In those days, Oregon had fertile farmlands, which were offered free to cultivators. Countless people trying to put lives of poverty in the East behind them and looking for a chance to attain wealth gathered at a town called Independence, east of Kansas City. They were brought there from the East via boats and other means.

West of Independence lay a wild, uncultivated region. The total distance from Independence to Oregon was 3,500 km. It was a journey that could

スから西は未開の荒野で、オレゴン州までの全行程は3,500km。家財道具や食料を積み込んだ牛車を引っぱって、1日15km前後しか進めない旅でした。なぜ、牛車だったのか。それは牛が野草を食べながらの厳しい旅にむいていたのと、いざとなれば食料としても使用できたからです。それは6ヵ月にのぼる、自然と戦い、ネイティブ・アメリカンから身を守りながらの旅でした。出発は春先。西部の山岳地帯を雪が降り出すまでに越えなければならなかったからです。

　当時、西部に旅立ったり、カリフォルニアのゴールドラッシュに参加したりして、アメリカのフロンティアに挑戦した人は数えきれません。春先にインディペンデンスから旅立った人々があまりにも多かったので、土煙があたりにもうもうと立ちこめたといいます。草原を西に向かう幌のついた車は、「草原のヨット」と呼ばれました。

Q　南北戦争とはどのような戦争だったんですか？

　南北戦争は、アメリカ東北部の経済発展によって取り残されていった南部の11州が、自らの経済を支えていた奴隷制を守ろうとして、アメリカ合衆国から脱退して引き起こした戦争です。

　南北戦争の時代は、すでに産業革命もかなり進行していました。従って、武器の精度もあがり、機関銃などが登場したのもこの時代のことです。

be advanced at only 15 km a day, since the travelers dragged oxcarts full of food and household belongings. They used oxcarts because oxen subsist on grass and were therefore good for the harsh journey, and they could become food in an emergency. The journey took six months: the travelers endured the hardships of nature and defended themselves against attacks from Native Americans. They left in spring because they had to cross the mountains in the West before the snow season.

In those days, countless people challenged the frontier, traveling to the West to take part in the California Gold Rush. So many people left Independence in the early spring that the area was said to be covered in a thick cloud of dust. Their covered wagons going west over the plains were called "prairie schooners."

Q What was the Civil War about?

The Civil War started when eleven Southern states, all of whom had been left behind economically by the Northeast, tried to secede from the USA in an attempt to keep hold of the system of slavery.

By this time, the industrial revolution had already progressed considerably. Consequently, weapon precision had increased and machine guns had been

南北戦争で最も激戦だったといわれるゲティスバーグの戦い

ところが、軍事戦略はそうした武器の変化に追い付いておらず、そのギャップが数多くの戦死者を出す原因となりました。1861年から65年までの4年間の戦争で、62万3,000人が死亡し、アメリカ史上最も大きな被害を出した戦争となりました。南部も北部もヨーロッパにまで広告を出し、国籍を与えることを条件に兵士を募集したほどです。

この戦争で、南部は結局北部に降伏しますが、その後南部は戦争のダメージで経済的に停滞し、その影響は20世紀になっても続いていきました。また、この戦争の結果、武力で連邦から脱退することは事実上不可能になり、アメリカはその後国を挙げて西部開拓へと向かうことになります。

南北戦争は、アメリカが最終的に一つとなり、国家として発展してゆく出発点となったアメリカ史上最も重要な出来事の1つだったのです。

Q いつ頃からカリフォルニアは発展を始めたのですか？

カリフォルニアを中心とした西海岸には17世紀からスペイン人の探検家が出入りし、少しずつ入植も行われていました。カリフォルニアの多くの土地がスペイン語の名前をつけられているのは、こうしたスペイン人の入植活動と、その後にカリフォルニアがメキシコ領となった名残です。

introduced. But there was a large gap between weaponry and strategy, which led to many fatalities in battle. In the four years from 1861 to 1865, 623,000 were killed—the greatest war casualties America had ever experienced. Both South and North openly recruited soldiers from Europe with the promise of granting them citizenship.

The South eventually surrendered, and the damage it sustained from the war had a deleterious effect on its economy well into the twentieth century. The war proved that it was impossible to secede from the confederation by force. Thereafter, the nation turned its full attention to development of the West.

The Civil War was one of the most important events in American history in that it was the starting point for all the states to come together to begin development as a nation.

Q When did development start in California?

The West Coast in and around California had been discovered and gradually settled by Spanish explorers in the seventeenth century. California has many Spanish place names, reminders of these Spanish settlements and of later Mexican occupation.

しかし、カリフォルニアに本格的に人々が住み始めたのは1848年にこの地で金が発見され、ゴールドラッシュが始まってからのことです。その後の10年間で、カリフォルニアには陸路と海路で何十万人もの入植者が入り込み、瞬く間にもともと住んでいたネイティブ・アメリカンやメキシコ系の人々を人口の上からも凌駕します。

　このように、アメリカの歴史上、未開の土地に人が入植することによって、現地の人々より入植者の方が多数となり、その結果その土地自体がアメリカになっていった例がいくつかあります。

　カリフォルニアも、1848年にメキシコとの戦争の結果アメリカ領になります。その後、こうした入植活動の結果、急速にアメリカ化が進められたのです。

　ちなみに、ゴールドラッシュに参加した人々のことを、ゴールドラッシュのピークとなった年(1849)を取って「フォーティナイナーズ」と呼びますが、これは現在サンフランシスコのアメリカン・フットボールのプロチームの愛称ともなっています。

ゴールドラッシュ時、金を採掘する老人

　以後、19世紀後半に大陸横断鉄道が開通すると、西海岸は急速に発展していきました。

Q　20世紀になってどうしてアメリカは大きく発展したのですか？

　20世紀になってアメリカが大きく発展したのは

However, it was only after 1848, when gold was discovered and the Gold Rush took place, that large populations began to settle in California. In ten years, hundreds of thousand of people came by land and sea to settle, overwhelming the Native Americans and Mexicans who had already made it their home.

This is only one example in American history where settlers moved into the wilderness and took it over, overwhelming the natives already living there through sheer numbers.

California became an American territory in 1848, as a consequence of the Mexican War. After that, it rapidly became Americanized as settler activity proceeded.

Incidentally, people who took part in the California Gold Rush are referred to as "Forty-Niners," after the year (1849) in which the Gold Rush reached its peak. Nowadays, the term is also the name of the San Francisco pro-football team.

The opening of the Transcontinental Railway accelerated West Coast development.

Q Why has America shown so much growth in the twentieth century?

The tremendous growth America has shown in the

いうまでもなくアメリカに渡ってきた膨大な移民やその子孫のパワーによるものです。19世紀だけで、アメリカの人口は14倍に膨れ上がり、20世紀初頭には7,600万人となりました。これらの人々がみな移民やその子孫としてアメリカの開拓に取り組んでいた人々なわけですから、そのパワーが想像されます。

彼らはできることなら貧困から抜け出して成功を自分の手でと、新しい事業や発明などに取り組みました。そうした努力が実を結び始めたのが20世紀初頭のことだったのです。その頃には、イギリスからカナダを経由してアメリカに渡ってきたグラハム・ベルの発明した電話が事業として拡大し、アメリカは通信産業で世界をリードする国となりました。

アメリカ発展の象徴、グラハム・ベルの発明した電話機

鯨とりから転身して自らの腕の入れ墨をロゴにして雑貨店を経営したメイシーズの店が19世紀に成功して、メイシーズ百貨店がニューヨークでさらに大きくなったのもこの頃でした。また、貧しい材木商の子供だったエジソンが、発明の才を活かし、その後20世紀の産業を引っぱっていく電気製品が次々と開発されたのもこの頃です。

こうしたアメリカン・ドリームが次々に結実し、成功した人々がさらに新しいアイデアに投資をし、

twentieth century is undoubtedly due to the spirit and energy of its huge number of immigrants and their offspring. In the nineteenth century alone, the North American population grew fourteen times to total 76 million at the start of the twentieth century. All those people were engaged in the development of the country, so their power was absolutely enormous.

They all made every effort to grasp success and pull themselves out of poverty with their own hands, engaging in new enterprises and inventions. It was at the beginning of the twentieth century that their efforts began to bear fruit. The invention of the telephone by Alexander Graham Bell, who had immigrated to the USA via Canada from England, led to the development of an enterprise. America gained leadership thereafter in the telecommunications industry.

Macy's department store developed in New York at the same time. Macy's was originally a successful general store run in the nineteenth century by an ex-whaler—he used the design of the tattoo on his arm as the store's logo. During this same period, Thomas Edison, the son of a poor lumber dealer with a brilliant talent for invention, developed a succession of electrical products that made the American electronics industry a leader in the twentieth century.

This kind of "American dream" continued to rapidly bear fruit. Successful people invested further money

アメリカ経済はどんどん成長していったのです。何か人と違ったことをして、チャンスをつかもうと懸命だったのです。これが、人にはないアイデアをどんどん売り込んで成功をというアメリカ独自の価値観を造りだします。

しかも、アメリカが着実に国家として成長していた19世紀末から20世紀前半といえば、ヨーロッパでは、旧来の王族による支配体制が揺れ、さらに各国の利権が対立し、内乱や戦争の絶えない時代でした。こうしたヨーロッパでの不安が相対的にアメリカの地位を上げていきます。

第1次世界大戦の頃には、アメリカは世界をリードする経済大国となっていたのです。

Q アメリカにとって第1次世界大戦はどのような戦争だったのですか？

第1次世界大戦は、ヨーロッパを壊滅させ、成長を続けてきたアメリカが、初めて世界に本格的な影響を与えた戦争でした。ドイツの無差別な潜水艦攻撃によってアメリカの艦船が被害を受けたことから、伝統的な孤立主義を破りヨーロッパの戦争に参戦した結果、アメリカは国際政治の上にも大きな影響力をもつようになりました。

しかし、戦後は再びアメリカは国際連盟に参加

in new ideas, which pushed the American economy to expand even more. People sought frantically to create opportunities by doing something that no one else was doing. This helped develop a particularly American attitude that one reaches success by promoting unique and totally original ideas.

During this period from the end of the nineteenth century to the early twentieth century while America was growing steadily, the various countries of Europe were either coming into conflict with one another or undergoing civil war as their old orders fell. Thus America's position rose as the situation in Europe became less stable.

By the time WWI broke out, America had become a world economic power.

Q What did WWI mean for the USA?

WWI brought devastation to Europe. But it also led the USA, now a mighty nation, to obtain a decisive influence over world events. The sinking of an American vessel by an all-out attack by a German submarine led the USA to revoke its stance of neutrality and participate in the war in Europe. Thus, the USA attained influential power in the international arena.

After the war, the USA remained outside the League

せず、ヨーロッパの政治から一歩引いた政策を続けていきます。とはいえ、当時アメリカは世界最大の債権国として、その経済は全世界のGDP（国内総生産）の25％弱を占めるまでになりました。アメリカは今日でも世界経済を大きく牽引する力を保ち続けているのです。

Q　アメリカはどのようにして第2次世界大戦に突入していったのですか？

エンパイア・ステート・ビル建築作業の様子

1929年のニューヨーク、ウォール街付近

　1929年に起きたウォール街の株の大暴落に端を発した大恐慌は、アメリカ経済に大打撃を与え、街は失業者で溢れます。

　しかし、それにもまして驚いたことは、このアメリカの大恐慌が世界に与えた打撃でした。この恐慌は、アメリカ経済が世界にインパクトを与える強大なものであることを皮肉にも証明したのです。そして、恐慌の最中でも、1931年にニューヨークにはエンパイア・ステート・ビルが完成し、ロックフェラー・センターが着工されました。また、サンフランシスコでは1933年にゴールデン・ゲート・ブリッジが着工され、その頃になると、大統領に就任したルーズベルトの指導力もあって、アメリカの経済は回復していきます。

　しかし、この恐慌を契機に、ヨーロッパや極東が再び不安定になっていったことは周知の事実で

of Nations and kept its distance from European politics. However, the USA was the world's largest creditor nation, and its economy comprised 25% of the world's GDP. The USA retains its dominant role in the world economy today.

Q What led the USA to join WWII?

The Great Depression, triggered by the stock-market crash on Wall Street in 1929, dealt a harsh blow to the USA. The streets teemed with unemployed workers.

What was more surprising was the blow the Depression dealt to the world at large. It proved that the American economy was so powerful it could send reverberations to other countries. Notwithstanding the Depression, however, in 1931 the Empire State Building was completed and construction began on the Rockefeller Center. In 1933, construction of the Golden Gate Bridge started in San Francisco. The American economy began to recover around this time under the leadership of President Theodore Roosevelt.

It is well known that the Depression brought instability to Europe and the Far East. When the USA took

しょう。特にアメリカは、日本の中国侵略に対して厳しい姿勢を貫き、日米関係は日々悪化していきました。また、ドイツによって引き起こされた戦争にも、イギリスと連携をとる形で対抗しようとします。

しかし、アメリカは、戦争当初は諸外国の動乱から距離をおき、自国の安全と繁栄を守ろうという意見が根強くあり、第2次世界大戦には直接は関与していなかったのです。そんなアメリカが戦争に巻き込まれたのは、他ならぬ、日本の参戦、すなわちハワイの真珠湾にあったアメリカ軍施設への奇襲攻撃だったのです。

Q ベトナム戦争はアメリカにどのような影響をもたらしたのですか？

ベトナム戦争で、多くのベトナム人難民がアメリカに移民した

ベトナム戦争は戦後の栄光を謳歌していたアメリカが、初めて大きくつまずいた戦争でした。パックス・アメリカーナを守ろうと他国に介入し、泥沼化した戦争の中で、多くの若者が命を失い、帰国できた人々の中にも深い傷を残しました。

今でも当時の心の傷が原因で、社会復帰できずに苦しむ帰還兵を街角などで見かけることがあります。ベトナム戦争は、アメリカの価値観が必ずしも世界から受け入れられないという現実を初め

a firm stance against the Japanese invasion of China, US-Japan relations worsened day by day. The USA also opposed the war started by Germany and built an alliance with England.

At the beginning of World War II, Americans held fast to their belief that their country should keep out of other nations' conflicts and look to her own security and prosperity. At this point, therefore, the USA was not directly involved. What brought the USA into the war was Japan's opening of hostilities—the sudden Japanese attack on the US military base in Pearl Harbor.

Q What impact did the Vietnam War have on the USA?

The Vietnam War was a war in which the USA, still reveling in its post-world-war glory, took its first bad stumble. Having intervened in the dispute of another country in an attempt to defend "Pax Americana," it became hopelessly mired, and a lot of young Americans lost their lives. The surviving veterans are still suffering deep wounds from that war.

Even now, one sometimes comes across veterans who are unable to return to normal social life due to psychological scars. It was the Vietnam War that made Americans realize for the first time that their values

て具体的な形でアメリカ人が理解した戦争でもありました。アメリカ国内での反戦運動を通して、以前は単純にアメリカは世界のリーダーだと思っていた人々までが、何で他国のことにアメリカがちょっかいを出す必要があるのかと政府に抗議したものです。

ベトナム戦争の後、アフガニスタンやイラクとの戦争まではアメリカ政府は世界の紛争への関わり方により慎重になり、アメリカの外交方針自体も大きく変化しました。アメリカ人一般の意識も、連邦政府へ懐疑心を抱く人や政治自体への無関心層が増え、アメリカ社会自体に変化をもたらしたのです。そして2001年の9/11は、一般のアメリカ人に多大な影響を与えることとなり、ベトナム戦争からの態度を一変させたのです。

アメリカの世論、アメリカ人気質

Q アメリカ人にとって最も人気のある大統領とは誰ですか？

ワシントン

独立戦争の英雄ジョージ・ワシントン（在職1789-1797）、黒人を解放し、南北戦争を戦ったエイブラハム・リンカーン（共和党 在職1861-1865）、内政外交両面でアメリカの役割を強固にした

were not necessarily shared by the rest of the world. In the anti-war movement within the states, even those people who had believed in the USA as a world leader protested against their government about its intervention in another country's affairs.

After the Vietnam War, and until the wars in Afganistan and Iraq, the US government became much more cautious about involvement in world conflicts and changed its diplomatic policy considerably. American public opinion itself changed, as many became suspicious of the federal government and others simply grew less interested in politics. The events of 9/11 in 2001 had an impact on American public opinion, shifting attitudes that had been in place from the Vietnam War.

USA Public Opinion and the American Disposition

Q Who were the most popular presidents in America?

The four most popular presidents in America are George Washington (years of office: 1789–1797), the hero of the War of Independence; Abraham Lincoln (Republican, 1861–1865), who liberated slaves and

セオドア・ルーズベルト

ケネディ

フランクリン・ルーズベルト

とされるセオドア・ルーズベルト（共和党 在職1901-1909）、キューバ危機を乗り切り、公民権運動を支持したジョン・F・ケネディ（民主党 在職1960-1963）の4人がアメリカで最も人気のある大統領とよく言われます。

そのほか、大恐慌のあとアメリカ経済を立て直し、第2次世界大戦を指導したフランクリン・ルーズベルト（民主党 在職1933-1945）、彼のあとを継いで第2次世界大戦を終結させ、戦後の世界体制を指導したハリー・トルーマン（民主党 在職1945-1953）、ベトナム戦争の後遺症や経済不況などに苦しんでいたアメリカ人に自信を復活させたロナルド・レーガン（共和党 在職1981-1989）などがアメリカ人が特に支持した大統領として知られています。

Q アメリカ人の日本観はどのように変化してきましたか？

初めて日本人がアメリカ人に広く紹介されたのは、1854年、ペリー提督による日本の開国のときでした。以来しばらくは、東洋のミステリアスな国の人々という漠然としたイメージが、アメリカ人にとっての日本観だったはずです。

しかし、その後ハワイや西海岸に日系人の移民

トルーマン

レーガン

fought the Civil War; Theodore Roosevelt (Republican, 1901–1909), who solodified the role of America in both domestic and international spheres; and John F. Kennedy (Democrat, 1960–1963), who weathered the Cuban Missile Crisis and approved civil rights.

Americans also favor Franklin Delano Roosevelt (Democrat 1933–1945), who rebuilt the American economy after the Great Depression and led the country in WWII; Harry S. Truman (Democrat, 1945–1953), who succeeded President Roosevelt, ended WWII, and had a leading hand in creating the world order after the war; and Ronald Reagan (Republican 1981–1989) who restored the self-confidence of Americans suffering from loss of pride after the Vietnam War and the recession.

Q How has the Americans' view of the Japanese changed?

Japan first became widely known in the USA after Commodore Perry brought an end to the country's seclusion. For a while the only image in the minds of most Americans was a vague one, that of a somewhat mysterious Oriental people.

Later, as Japanese immigrants came and settled in

が上陸し、実際に現地の人々と生活を共にするようになると、職をめぐる争いなどに端を発して、偏見や差別が横行するようになりました。とはいえ、政治的には日露戦争の頃までは日本とアメリカとは友好関係にあったことはよく知られています。しかし、その後アジアに対する利害の対立などから、次第に両者は反目し、その結果第2次世界大戦となったことは周知の事実です。

　戦争中、日系人の多くは強制収容所での生活を余儀なくされます。こうしたアメリカ国内での差別に対して、1988年にはアメリカの政府が陳謝し、収容所に入れられた人々への補償も行われました。

　さて、アメリカの日本人観は戦後大きく変化します。特に戦後に日本を訪れた人々の中から知日派と呼ばれるアメリカ人も増え、日本の経済復興と共に日米間の民間レベルでの交流も活発になりました。

　しかし、1980年代に入って、日本経済が大きくなり、アメリカと本格的に交流するようになると、政治の上では貿易摩擦が、民間レベルでは日米双方のビジネス文化の違いから来る摩擦が増えてきたのもまた事実です。

　現在、アメリカ人からみても、日本人からみても、お互いは友好国でありながら、どことなく分かり

Hawaii and the West Coast, prejudice and discrimination against them became rampant, mainly originating in disputes over jobs. At the diplomatic level, Japan and the USA had amicable relations until after the Japanese-Russo War (which took place in 1904–05). Thereafter that, however, the two countries became antagonistic due to conflicts in their interests in Asia. This was one factor that eventually led to their clash in WWII.

During WWII, most Japanese-Americans were sent to relocation camps, something for which the US government offered an official apology in 1988—acknowledging discrimination and giving compensation to those who underwent such treatment by their own country.

After WWII, Americans' views of the Japanese changed dramatically. The number of Americans who visited Japan after the war and reacted favorably increased. As the Japanese economy recovered, exchanges on a civilian level began to take place.

However, in the 1980s, as the Japanese economy swelled, and full-scale exchange with the USA started, outbreaks of trade and cultural friction occurred.

Nowadays, most Americans and Japanese seem to think of their countries as having friendly relations,

づらい国だという意識を持った人が増えているようです。特に、最近のアジア経済の活況は、アメリカ人の目をただ日本だけに向けるのではなく、日本をアジアの中のパートナーの1つと位置付ける考え方も目立ってきました。

Q アメリカ人にとって最も大切な価値観とは何ですか？

アメリカ人が培ってきた最も大切な価値観とは、おそらく「インディビジュアリズム」、すなわち個人主義という価値観でしょう。自らを信じ、自らの責任で物事を成し遂げていく強い意志を表します。

また、「インディビジュアリズム」のかわりに「インディペンデンス」（独立心）や「フリーダム」（自由）を大切な価値だとする人も多くいます。

さらに未来をみつめ変化を受け入れ、常に新しい事柄に挑戦しようとする価値観もアメリカ人にとっては貴重なものです。こうした価値観を「オプティミズム」（楽天主義）といいます。

面白いことに、この「インディビジュアリズム」も「オプティミズム」も、日本人からみるとそれほど前向きで良い価値観とは解釈されていません。ここにアメリカ人と日本人との文化背景の違いによる、意識の差異をみてとれそうです。

despite some differences that each finds difficult to understand. The recent economic boom in other Asian countries has drawn Americans' attention away from Japan alone, and led to a new appraisal of Japan as just one of America's trading partners within Asia.

Q What is the most important American value?

The most important value nurtured by Americans is probably "individualism"—a strong belief in oneself and the determination to achieve something through one's own actions.

Other important values might include "independence" and "freedom," which are equally valued by many people.

Yet another important American value is "optimism"—looking toward the future, accepting change, and always trying new things.

Interestingly, neither "individualism" nor "optimism" hold quite such positive value for the Japanese. That difference between Americans and Japanese is probably based on their different cultural backgrounds.

◆コラム◆ パールハーバーとアメリカ

　大統領の任期最後の年に、オバマ大統領が広島を訪れ、被爆者を見舞ったことは、日本人に好感情を与えました。しかし、アメリカには、太平洋戦争当時、頑なに戦争を遂行していた日本の軍部を壊滅させるためには原爆の投下は仕方がなかったという意見が根強く残っています。原爆を投下しなければ、戦争の終結は遅れ、それ以上の犠牲者がでたはずだというのです。

　そんなアメリカの世論を考えたとき、日本の安部首相がパールハーバーを訪れたことは大きな意義がありました。太平洋戦争はアメリカ海軍の基地があるパールハーバーを日本が不意打ちしたことから始まったために、アメリカには宣戦布告もせずにいきなり攻撃をしかけてきた日本への敵意が長い間残っていたからです。

　アメリカの歴史を振り返れば、アメリカが独立して以来、アメリカの領土が直接攻撃を受けたのは1812年にイギリス軍がワシントンD.C.を占領した時と、このパールハーバーの事件以外にはなかったのです。

　それだけに、2001年9月11日に、ニューヨークの貿易センタービルなどがテロ攻撃の標的となったことは、パールハーバー以来の衝撃となりました。今ではセプテンバーイレブンといえば、このテロ攻撃のことを指し、アメリカ人はパールハーバーと同様に、この日のことを長く記憶に留めようとしているのです。

　とはいえ、パールハーバーとヒロシマが共に過去の歴史の事件として記録され、人々の敵意や憎しみとは離れた出来事となるにはまだ時間と努力が必要です。しかし、2016年に両国の指導者が太平洋戦争を象徴するこの2つの場所をそれぞれ訪問したことは、日本とアメリカが未来に向けて友好を深める意味では、重要なステップだったのかもしれません。

Chapter 3
American Politics

第3章　アメリカの政治

アメリカの民主主義

Q 連邦政府と地方政府との関係はどのようになっているのですか？

アメリカ大統領の印章

　アメリカは基本的に地方政府の力が強い国です。各州には州憲法があり、法律があります。連邦政府の役割は、貨幣の鋳造など、州単位では決定できない種類の内政、外交そして軍事を行うわけですが、その機能自体は日本の政府機関よりはかなり小さくなっています。各地方が自らの判断でなし得ることで、合衆国憲法に抵触しないものであれば、それはその地方の判断に大幅にゆだねられているのです。

　1994年には、議会と大統領との対立がもとで、国家予算が通過せず国のサービスが中断したことがありました。しかし、このとき影響が出たのは、国立公園のサービス停止や、パスポートの発給など特定の状況におかれた人だけで、一般の生活には支障はなかったといいますから、いかに連邦政府が一般国民とは遠いところにある存在か理解できます。

　ただし、南北戦争から現在に至る社会の変化の中で、次第に連邦政府の役割が強くなり、昔はあ

American Democracy

Q What is the relationship between state and federal governments?

America is basically a country where state governments have a lot of power. Each state has its own constitution and laws. It is the federal government's role to execute domestic affairs that cannot be decided on the state level, such as the minting of money, and to decide diplomatic and military affairs. The functions of the US federal government are thus considerably smaller than those of the Japanese government. State governments handle all those matters that are possible to handle under their own jurisdiction—as long as they do not involve matters to do with the US Constitution.

In 1994, due to the deadlock between the Congress and the president at the time, Bill Clinton, Congress could not pass a national budget and federal services were suspended. But the only way in which the public was affected was in the closure of national parks and the suspension of passport issuance. This demonstrates how distant the federal government is from the lives of the general public.

Despite this, the role of the federal government has become stronger gradually, due to various social

たかも独立国のようだったそれぞれの州が、次第に国家の一部として機能するようになってきたのも事実です。

1995年の冬にオクラホマ・シティで連邦政府のビルが爆破された事件がありました。実はこの犯人たちはだんだん強くなってきた連邦政府が個人の生活に影響を及ぼすことを極端に嫌う民兵組織の反抗だったといわれています。

アメリカでは今でもときどき、連邦政府の枠から離れて自らの町や村を自立させようという動きがあるのです。

Q 民主党と共和党はそれぞれどのような背景を持った党なのですか？

民主党のシンボル、ロバ

共和党のシンボル、象

民主党と共和党は、アメリカの二大政党として議会を二分しています。民主党のシンボルマークはロバで、もともとは強い政府に反対し、地方の権利を主張する政党として活動していました。共和党のシンボルはゾウで、独立戦争の後の強い政府を樹立しようとした人々にそのルーツを追うことができ、リンカーンの下で奴隷解放運動を進めていったのも共和党です。

しかし、20世紀になって、この構図が逆転しました。アメリカの資本主義の隆盛と共に、共和党は自由競争を支持する立場から、企業の利益を保

changes that have taken place since the Civil War. State governments, once almost like independent countries, have begun to function more as a part of a nation.

The bombing of the Murrah federal government building in Oklahoma City in the winter of 1995 is an extreme example of some people's opposition of the federal government. The accused in this case were members of militia groups that abhor the federal government's interference in the life of the individual.

Throughout the USA, many people are intent on gaining independence from the federal government for their towns and villages.

Q What is the history behind the Democratic and Republican Parties?

The Democrats and Republicans are the two major parties constituting the American Congress. The Democratic Party, whose mascot is a donkey, was originally a party opposed to strong government and for regional rights. The Republican Party, whose mascot is an elephant, originally supported strong government after the War of Independence and promoted emancipation of slaves under President Lincoln.

In the twentieth century, this structure was reversed. With the rise of American capitalism, the Republican Party began to protect corporate benefits in keeping

護する立場をとっていきます。それに対して民主
党は、組合などと連携しながら、政府が経済をコ
ントロールし、資本主義の行き過ぎを押さえよう
とする立場をとったのです。

　特に大恐慌以降、政府による計画経済でアメリ
カ経済を活性化させた民主党は、その後も強い政
府を主張する立場をとり続けてきました。

　また、共和党はそれに対して伝統的なアメリカ
の価値を前面に押し出し、自由競争、小さな政府
を主張し、その政策論争は1990年代にクリントン
政権と議会で僅差ながら多数を占める共和党との
対立にも象徴的に現れています。

　さらに、ヒラリー・クリントンに対抗して大統
領候補戦に立候補したバーニー・サンダースなど、
二大政党以外からの候補者が大きな支持を集めま
した。サンダースは民主党の党員でもありません
でした。また政治慣れしたワシントンD.C.の候補
者を批判する反体制派として、2016年の大統領選
に勝利したのは、ドナルド・トランプでした。

　民主党も共和党も巨大な政党です。しかも、こ
うした長い歴史的な経緯を経ているだけに、党内
にも様々な立場の人がいて、党を１つにまとめて

with their support of free competition. Conversely, the Democratic Party supported government control over the economy in order to restrain excess capitalism and collaborated with labor unions.

The Democratic Party has continued to make a case for strong government, especially after the Great Depression. They were the party, after all, that revived the American economy through government planning at this time.

The Republican Party, on the other hand, promulgated traditionally American values, supporting free competition and small government. Such policy disagreements emerged symbolically in the confrontation between the Clinton administration and the Republican Party who held a thin majority in Congress during the 1990s.

More recently, candidates from outside the mainstream have garnered widespread public support, including Bernie Sanders (who was not a registered member of the Democratic Party but ran a heated campaign against Hillary Clinton), and Donald Trump, who succeeded in the 2016 presidential campaign as an anti-establishment candidate critical of "politics as usual" in Washington, DC.

Both parties are enormous. Also, because of the long history behind them, their members have diversified backgrounds, and this sometimes makes a unified

アメリカ人実業家、ロス・ペロー

アメリカの弁護士で社会運動家、ラルフ・ネーダー

いくのもかなり大変です。アメリカではこうした二大政党政治が硬直しているとして、新たな政治の在り方を模索しようとする声もあがっています。1990年代に、2度にわたって大統領選挙に立候補したロス・ペローなどは、そうした第3の勢力として注目を集めました。2000年になると、グリーンの党を率いるラルフ・ネーダーが大統領選に出馬し、第3の政党として注目を集めました。

Q アメリカの選挙システムはどのようになっているのですか？

アメリカでは、18歳以上のアメリカ市民への選挙権が保障されています。選挙人名簿への登録が本人の自主性に任されているのもアメリカの選挙システムの特徴といえそうです。

各地域コミュニティでの選挙にはじまって国政選挙まで、アメリカには数えきれないほどの選挙がありますが、国政の場合は、上院は各州から2名を選び、6年の任期が与えられています。また、下院は人口に比例し定員が定められ、議員の任期は2年です。

こうした通常の選挙と共に、大切なのが4年に1度の大統領選挙です。これは有権者が選挙人を選び、選挙人が大統領候補に投票をするという間接選挙の形をとっています。また大統領選挙から

position difficult. There are some people who would like to find another way of doing politics—they consider the two existing parties to be stagnant. Ross Perot, who ran in two presidential elections in the 1990s, drew much attention for his influence as an independent third party. Ralph Nader, who was a presidential candidate representing the Green Party in the 2000 election has attracted similar attention for third-party politics.

Q How does the electoral system work?

In the USA, any citizen over eighteen years old has guaranteed voting rights. One characteristic of the American voting system is that voter registration is voluntary.

Various elections take place in the USA—from local community elections to those on a national government level. Two senators for national government are elected from each state with six-year terms. For the House of Representatives, or Congress, there is a quorum in proportion to each state's population, and each representative's term is two years.

The most important election is the presidential election, conducted every four years. This is actually an indirect election in which voters vote for electors who in turn vote for the candidate. The election of members

2008年共和党の全国党大会の様子

2年目に行われる議員や多くの州知事が選ばれる選挙を特に中間選挙と呼び、その後の政局を占う上でも重要な選挙であるとされています。

Q アメリカの大統領はどのような役割を担っているのですか？

大統領はアメリカの国家元首です。従って、単に行政の長というだけでなく、アメリカという国家の頂点に立つシンボルでもあるのです。業務としては、閣僚を任免し自らの政治理念に従って政策を遂行します。また、軍隊の最高責任者として陸海空3軍を統帥し、有事には交戦や和平についての決断を行うのも大統領の仕事です。

議会に対しては、法律の制定を促したり、議会の決議した法案を拒否したりする権限も持っています。

このように、大統領は日本の総理大臣と比べれば、かなり強大な権限を持っています。しかし、大統領は任期が終わればただの人です。また、4年すれば再選されるかどうか国民の審判を受けなければなりません。従って、強大な権力を持つ大統領は、常に国民の世論に気を配り、適切なアドバイスをくれる側近の助言に耳を傾けているのです。

of Congress and governors, conducted every second year after the presidential election, is called an off-year election and is an important indicator in forecasting the political situation.

Q What is the role of the president of the United States of America?

The president is the national chief of the USA. Not only is he the chief of the government, but he also has a symbolic role as the head of the nation. The president nominates Cabinet members and carries out policies based on his political beliefs. As "Commander in Chief," he commands the army, navy, marine corps, and air force, and he carries the final decision on war or ceasefires.

As regards Congress, the president has the power to urge members to pass laws, and he can also veto bills that have passed through Congress.

The US president thus has stronger powers than the Japanese prime minister. At the end of his term (if he is not re-elected), he returns to civilian life. It is up to the nation whether to re-elect a president at the end of his four-year term. Despite the strong power with which he is vested, the president therefore has to pay continual attention to public opinion, and take heed of advice from his close associates.

Q 大統領と議会の役割、そして関係はどのようになっているのですか?

ワシントンD.C.にあるアメリカの議事堂

2016年の大統領選に勝利したのは共和党で、同じく議会の多数派も共和党です。以前は大統領が共和党の時に、議会は民主党が多数派であることが普通でした。このように、議会と大統領とが常に牽制しあう構造が長年続いているのです。

これは民主主義の大原則である三権分立の原則からみても健全なあり方であるといえるかもしれません。

ただ、大統領に投票をした同じ国民が、大統領の所属する政党とは反対の立場をとる政党を多数党に選ぶ背景には、年と共に増大する社会不安や貧困への恐怖に有効な手立てを打ち出せない行政や議会への不満や苛立ちがあるのだという見方をする人もいます。実際、激しく動く世の中や、国際政治、あるいは経済の高低によって、人々の政治への見方が右から左へ、あるいは左から右へ落ち着きなく振れるのが、現在のアメリカの有権者の傾向です。もちろん、行政も議会も１つの政党に固められ、政治が極端に左右に揺れることを嫌う国民感情がそうした選挙結果に現れるのも事実でしょう。

いずれにせよ、大統領が法案を拒否したり、大統領の政策が議会にそっぽを向かれたりと、なか

Q What are the roles of the US president and Congress, and how are they related?

The US president elected in 2016 is a Republican, and the majority in the US Congress is Republican. Previously, it was common for the presidents to be Republicans with the majority of Congress Democrats. The system of checks and balances provided by the structure of government has thus been ongoing.

This is probably a sound procedure from the viewpoint of the separation of the three powers (which are judicial, legislative, and executive), the major principle of democracy.

There are some people, however, who criticize this way of doing things: they say people who vote for a president from one party vote for the opposite party as the majority party simply out of growing dissatisfaction and irritation when government and Congress cannot seem to take effective measures against social instability and poverty. As the world changes and international politics and economies fluctuate, American voters' political views tend to shift in one direction and then another. Of course, such election returns might also be a reflection of the American dislike of extreme shifts to the right or left, foreseeable in the case of an administration and Congress of the same party.

At all events, a major problem in the relations between the present president and Congress is the

なか物事が進まないのも、現在の大統領と議会との関係における最大の問題点でもあるのです。

Q ブッシュ政権のことをアメリカ人をどう思っているのですか？

　9月11日（2001年）にアメリカ同時多発テロ事件が起き、アメリカは急激に保守化しました。事件以降、ジョージ・W・ブッシュは、アフガニスタンやイラクとの戦争に突き進みました。強いアメリカが、その経済力や軍事力を使って世界に平和をもたらすことができると考えたのです。この考え方を「新保守主義」と言います。アフガニスタン戦争で囚われた捕虜たちは、キューバのグアンタナモにあるキャンプに収容され、そこで拷問されていたという証拠が出たのです。これにより、テロへの戦いの正当性に暗い影を落としたのです。

　世界中が、ブッシュ政権は国際法と、超大国としてのアメリカのニーズのどちらにプライオリティを置いたのか、と訝（いぶか）りはじめたのです。

　外交政策、そしてブッシュ政権末期の経済の落ち込みへの批判が高まったことが大きな要因となり、保守的な立場を堅持しようとする共和党の人気は下降していきました。8年にわたるブッシュ政権が終わると、共和党は敗北し、民主党のバラク・オバマ政権が誕生したのです。

第43代米大統領ジョージ・W・ブッシュ。同時多発テロ後、世界的なテロとの戦いを押し進めた

slow rate of progress in passing bills: the president has either used his veto, or Congress has refused outright to support his policies.

Q What did people think of the Bush Administration?

The 9/11 terrorist attacks caused America to suddenly become more right wing, and George W. Bush subsquently led the country into wars against Afghanistan and Iraq. In Bush's vision, a strong America would use its economic and military power to bring stability to the world. This idea is referred to as "Neoconservatism." Prisoners from the war in Afghanistan were interred at the Guantanamo military base on the island of Cuba, and there is evidence that people were tortured there. This certainly cast a shadow over the legitimacy of the War on Terror.

The world began to wonder whether the Bush Administration was putting priority on international law or America's needs as a superpower.

Criticism of its foreign policy and the economic recession at the end of Bush's term were major reasons for the staunchly conservative Republican Party's loss of popularity. After eight years of George Bush's government, the Republicans were defeated, and Barack Obama's Democratic administration took over.

Q　バラク・オバマが選ばれたのはなぜなのでしょうか？

　2008年、アメリカ国民は、イラク戦争の成り行きを心配し、かつリーマン・ショック後の経済の不透明さや失業率に気を揉んでいました。こうした問題山積の時期、国民は抜本的な政治改革を熱望し、そこに乗じて民主党は「チェンジ(Change)」という言葉をスローガンにしたのです。民主党はあっけなく勝利を収め、2009年、バラク・オバマが新大統領に就任しました。オバマはアメリカ史上初の黒人大統領で、かつハワイ生まれ初の国家の最高職責を担う人になったのです。

　当時、オバマ政権は、最悪の経済状況に立ち向かわなければならず、その上、アフガニスタンやイラクとの戦争も続いていました。財政赤字も増加していました。そんな中、「チェンジ」を実行するのは非常に困難で、支持率の点でも厳しい状況が続いたのです。

　しかし、2011年になると景気回復の兆しが見えはじめました。さらにイラクからはほとんどの軍隊が撤退し、同時多発テロの首謀者オサマ・ビン・ラディンも暗殺されたのです。こうしたことがオバマへの追い風となりました。

　2期目に入ったオバマ政権は、顕著な成果をいくつかあげました。国民健康保険の設置、経済成長の継続、それに合わせた失業率の低下などです。

Q What brought about the election of Barack Obama?

In 2008, Americans were worried about the war in Iraq, and also about unemployment and economic uncertainty that were caused by the Lehman Shock. In these difficult times, people were demanding fundamental political reforms, and the Democratic Party adopted the word "Change" as its slogan. The Democrats won easily, and Barack Obama was inaugurated as president in 2009. Obama became the first African-American president in the history of America and was also the first person born in Hawaii to be elected to America's highest office.

The Obama administration faced the worst economic situation in recent years, a serious unemployment problem, and on top of that, there were the wars in Afghanistan and Iraq, and the budget deficit was also increasing. It was difficult to implement change, and it has been an uphill battle in terms of his support ratings.

However, in 2011, the economy began to show signs of recovery, most troops were withdrawn from Iraq, and Osama Bin Laden, the mastermind behind the 9/11 terrorist attacks was assassinated, which has increased Obama's appeal with voters.

Although the Obama Administration achieved a number of notable achievements in its second term, including a shift in healthcare policy and several

ただ、こうしたことはミドルクラスの人たちの状況を変えることにはつながらなかったのです。この批判的なムードをうまく捉えたのがドナルド・トランプでした。それにより、オバマ時代の政策をほぼ引き継ぐと思われていたアメリカ女性初の大統領候補は落選し、政治の経験のないドナルド・トランプが2016年の大統領選に勝利することになるのです。

アメリカの法体系と人権

Q 合衆国憲法はどのような特徴をもっていますか？

合衆国憲法の第1ページ目

合衆国憲法への署名シーン

合衆国憲法は1787年に発議され、その翌年に発効されました。憲法には、民主主義国家としての議会の運営や大統領の権限など、様々な項目がありますが、アメリカの憲法で特に注目したいのは、憲法の条文のあとに年を追って付け加えられた修正事項です。

修正事項の作成は1791年にまず行われました。そこでは、例えば居住者の承認や法的な手続きなしに、軍隊が個人の住居を接収でき

years of solid economic growth, matched by declining unemployment, there was also a sense that he had not been successful in improving the status of the middle class. This critical mood was skillfully captured by the Trump campaign, so instead of electing America's first woman president, who was seen as "more of the same" representing policies from the Obama presidency, the political outsider, Donald Trump, succeeded in winning the 2016 presidential election.

The Judicial System and Human Rights

Q What are the characteristics of the US Constitution?

The US Constitution was proposed in 1787 and promulgated the following year. It is composed of many articles stipulating such things as how to run the Congress of a democratic nation, the power of the president, and so forth. Amendments later added to the articles of the Constitution are particularly important.

The first amendments were made in 1791 and included the following additions: No soldier could be quartered in any house without the consent of the

ないこと（修正第３項）とか、よく統率のとれた民兵を組織したり、武器を持つ権利を保障する（修正第２項）といった条項が加えられました。当時はアメリカがイギリスの圧政から独立を勝ち取ったばかりだったため、再び国民が圧政や専制政治に苦しまないようにと、わざわざこうした修正事項が付け加えられたのです。

また、独立戦争はイギリスからみれば不法行為でした。従って、当時のアメリカ人は自らが国家によって裁かれるときの個人の権利に対して大変敏感で、例えば、過度な保釈金や罰金を禁じたり（修正第８項）、自らのコミュニティが選んだ陪審員によって裁判を受ける権利（修正第６項）など罪を犯した人の人権についての項目が付加されました。

ちなみに、大統領の３回以上の再選を禁じたのは1951年の修正（修正第22項）で、その他にも時代によって人々の権利関係が複雑になるにつれ、様々な事項が付け加えられたのです。

合衆国憲法の基本理念は、基本的な人権の保障と、権力の均衡と分散、そして民主主義の保障という大きな柱で成り立っています。そして、この理念は1776年に発表された独立宣言の趣旨に基づいています。特に独立宣言の前半に記されている、「全ての人間は平等であることは自明の理であり、人々が生命、自由、幸福の追求を求める権利は神

owner (Amendment III); every person has the right to organize a well-regulated militia and to bear arms (Amendment II). These amendments were made just after America attained independence from England, to prevent the nation ever falling under the rule of despotism again.

The War of Independence was an unlawful act from England's point of view, which made Americans extremely sensitive to individual rights in national trials. The following amendments regarding the human rights of criminals were made: excessive bail and excessive fines are prohibited (Amendment VIII); every person who has committed a crime has a right to trial by an impartial jury chosen from a community of his or her peers.

A further amendment made in 1951, Amendment XXII, prohibits the president from being elected to office more than twice. Various amendments were thus added as issues concerning rights became more complicated over time.

The underlying principles of the US Constitution consist of the protection of fundamental human rights, the balance and separation of powers, and the guarantee of democracy. These principles are based on the spirit of the Declaration of Independence. The ideas behind the affirmation "that all men are created equal, that they are endowed by their Creator with certain

が保障したもので、それを確保するために政府が存在する」という意図の文章が、憲法採択の主旨ともなったもので、そうした人権を維持するために、修正事項が付け加えられたのです。

従って、1791年の修正事項の最後に加えられた、この憲法で定められなかった権利は全てそれぞれの州の権利、あるいは個人の権利として保全する（修正第10項）という内容の一文は、特に個人の自由や地方政府の自治を強く保障した条文として注目されるのです。

Q　公民権とはどのような権利のことですか？

公民権というのは、アメリカに住む人が差別なく市民として同様の権利を享受できる権利を指しています。独立宣言には全ての「人」は平等に創造されているという一文があります。この「人」が誰を意味するのかということが、アメリカでの公民権の確立の歴史といえるのです。独立戦争当時は白人男性の、しかも資産を所有する人だけに平等が保障されていました。それが、南北戦争を通してまず奴隷が解放され、男女同権が確立し、その後あらゆる人への平等の原則が確立したのです。

この公民権を確立させる運動を公民権運動といいますが、それが最も激しく展開されたのが1955

unalienable Rights, that among these are Life, Liberty and the pursuit of Happiness, that to secure these rights, Governments are instituted among Men," became the mainstay of the Constitution. The Amendments were made in order to protect those human rights.

The last part of the Amendments made in 1791 specifies that "The powers not delegated to the United States by the Constitution, nor prohibited by it to the States, are reserved to the States respectively, or to the people." (Amendment X). This Article strongly guarantees the individual freedom and the autonomy of state governments.

Q What are "civil rights"?

Civil rights are the rights that all people living in the USA are given equally as citizens. In the Declaration of Independence, there is a phrase that "all men are created equal." The question of who these "men" are embodies the history of American civil rights. At the time of the American Revolution, only white men who owned property were guaranteed equality. Slaves were liberated after the Civil War, and later, equal rights for both sexes and the principle of equality for all were established.

The struggle to establish civil rights is called the civil rights movement. It was most intense from 1955

黒人を差別する待合室の看板

黒人専用の映画館の入り口

年から60年代中盤までで、連邦政府の指導とキング牧師などの活動によって、職場やホテルやレストランなどの商業施設、公共施設などでのあらゆる差別の撤廃と、偏見や暴力に対する人権の擁護が法制化され、1964年に施行されたのです。

現在、この公民権法は、アメリカの原点を守る法律として、あたかも憲法と同じように厳しく運用され、不当な差別に対しては民事のみならず時には重い刑罰が適用されています。

Q アメリカ人の偏見や差別に対抗する活動にはどのようなものがありますか？

アメリカでの平等に関する感覚を象徴しているのが、頻繁に行われている役職名の表記の変更ではないでしょうか。

例えば、チェアマンは、マンが男だけを指す言葉だとして、チェアパーソンに、同様に郵便配達をする人を意味するメイルマン（郵便配達人）はメイルパーソンに、さらにはミスとミセスの使い分けをやめてミズと統一したり、オリエンタルという言葉が昔の東洋に対するステレオタイプを象徴するとして、アジアン（エージアン）に変更されるなど、例を挙げればきりがありません。日本でもこうした表記の変更はありますが、アメリカはその上をいっているようです。

to the mid-1960s. In 1964, under the direction of the federal government and through the activities of leaders like Martin Luther King, Jr., a law was established to abolish segregation and discrimination on grounds of race, and to protect people from prejudice and violence.

Currently, civil rights laws are enforced strictly, much like the Constitution, as laws that protect the founding principles of the USA. Unfair discrimination not only becomes the subject of civil law suits—very heavy penalties can also be imposed.

Q What do Americans do to counteract prejudice and discrimination?

The widespread changes that have taken place in official titles symbolizes Americans' sensibility regarding issues of equality.

The "man" of "chairman," for example, refers only to males, so this title has been changed to "chairperson." Similarly, "mailman" has been changed to "mailperson," "Miss" and "Mrs." to "Ms.," and "Oriental" to "Asian" (since the word Oriental evokes a stereotyped image). Such changes are made in Japan too, nowadays, but not as frequently as in the USA.

こうした傾向を受け、1980年代にはアファーマティブ・アクションがしきりと話題になりました。

アファーマティブ・アクションとは、公民権法によって保障された平等の原則を徹底させるために、もともと差別が横行していたことから社会の上でハンディキャップを背負わされた人々に大学や企業、そして公共施設への就職に有利な条件を与え、社会へ進出するチャンスを与えようという考えのもとに制定された法律のことです。

具体的には、大学に入学する規準を、黒人などの特定のマイノリティには緩くしたり、就職のための特定の採用枠を設定したりといった制度を指しています。例えば、企業の場合、アファーマティブ・アクションを遵守し積極的に運用した企業には、連邦政府や州政府が優先的に注文を出したりといった奨励策も打ち出されました。

しかし、このアファーマティブ・アクションは逆に機会に対する平等の原則に反し、逆差別を生むものだという批判も多かったのです。カリフォルニア州では以前の共和党の州知事、ピート・ウィルソンがアファーマティブ・アクションを撤廃したケースも起こりました。1996年のことです。2010年、カリフォルニア州の最高裁判所は再度この決定を承認しました。

アファーマティブ・アクションは、何が本当の平等かというテーマをめぐり争点となっている法律でもあるのです。

公民権運動の指導者、キング牧師

Affirmative action widely debated in the 1980s, was a reflection of these trends.

Affirmative action is a system established under the law to underpin the principle of equality guaranteed by civil rights laws. It promotes opportunities for minorities to advance in society by providing advantageous conditions for college enrollment, as well as company and public job employment to persons from historically disadvantaged groups or groups that have suffered discrimination.

Under this system, conditions required for college enrollment are moderated or a special employment framework is created for employment. Companies that practice affirmative action are encouraged in various ways—for example, they can be given preferential treatment from federal and state government when orders are placed.

Affirmative action laws are sometimes criticized as contradicting the principle of equal opportunity and creating reverse discrimination. The then-Republican governor of California, Pete Wilson, abolished affirmative action in that state in 1996. Again in 2010, the California Supreme Court upheld the ban.

A controversy as to what true equality means continues to surround the issue of affirmative action.

Q アメリカの裁判制度はどのような特徴がありますか？

アメリカ政府の司法を統括する最高裁判所

アメリカでの裁判は多くの場合、陪審員の評決に基づいて行われます。陪審員は、被告が有罪か無罪かを評決し、その結果をもとに裁判長が量刑を言い渡すのが習わしです。これは、イギリス以来の伝統に加え、自分たちの住む地域の意思をできるだけ裁判にも反映させようという、アメリカならではの考え方によって維持されている制度です。しかし細かく見てみると、アメリカの裁判制度、訴追や量刑に関する規定は州によって異なります。また、金融関係や広域犯罪など、連邦政府が関与する刑事事件などでは、連邦政府の裁判所が審理を行います。

まず、被告は法廷で裁かれるのかどうか、大陪審の評決を受けます。そしてその評決に基づいて、裁判所でさらに陪審員が事件を審理し、法的なアドバイスを裁判所から受けながら、有罪か無罪かを評決するのです。

陪審員は裁判所が選挙人名簿などから選び、市民は陪審員になる義務を有します。ただ、被告人にとってあきらかに不利な陪審員がいる場合は、弁護士はその陪審員の忌避を裁判所に求めることもでき、そうした駆け引きも裁判での大切なプロセスの1つとなります。

裁判では、弁護士と検事が、被告を守る立場と追及する立場とに分かれ、論戦を繰り広げますが、

Q What are the characteristics of the US trial system?

In the USA most judgments are made based on jury verdict. The jury delivers a verdict of guilty or not guilty, and the judge gives a judgment accordingly. This system is based on the British tradition but maintained with a very American sense of doing justice to the will of the community. A closer look shows that provisions for the trial system, prosecution, and judgment differ from state to state. Finance-related cases, crimes affecting a wide area, and criminal cases involving the federal government are tried in federal court.

First, the defendant accepts the Grand Jury verdict of whether or not he or she is to be tried at court. The jury then tries the case accordingly with legal advice from the court, and brings in a verdict of guilty or not guilty.

The jury is selected by the court using voting lists and other means. Citizens are obliged by law to do jury duty. If a juror is obviously biased for or against the defendant, the lawyer can plead that he or she be dismissed. Such bargaining is an important part of the trial process.

During the trial, the defense and prosecution lawyers conduct a fight with words. The two sides defend and

これもいかに陪審員を説得するかを目的とした行為です。アメリカでは一度無罪となれば検察側は控訴できません。それだけに、陪審員に対する説得に両者はしのぎを削るのです。

Q　アメリカでの司法取り引きとはどのようなものですか？

司法取り引きとは、捜査に協力したり、罪を認め検事に協力したりした被告が減刑されるという考え方です。これは制度でも何でもなく、検事に協力したからといって、必ず有利な判決を得られるという保証はどこにもありません。

ただ、ギャング・グループなどの広域で複雑な犯罪に対して、被告人の1人が捜査に協力することで、もっと重大な事件の犯人を起訴できたりするのも事実です。そうした時に、検事は裁判所に働きかけ、情状酌量を求めるわけです。

実際に、ニューヨークのマフィアのボスが終身刑を受けた裁判で、捜査に協力した殺人犯が短い禁固刑の後に釈放された事例など、司法取り引きが行われたケースはたくさん存在しています。

Q　アメリカには死刑はないのですか？

アメリカは州によって死刑を認めている州と、

prosecute the defendant, and try to persuade the jury their way. In America, if a defendant is judged not guilty, prosecutors cannot appeal, and this causes both sides to put up a furious fight.

Q What is legal bargaining in the USA?

Legal bargaining involves the reduction of penalties for cooperation in criminal investigations, or cooperation with prosecutors by confessing the crime. This is not a system per se, and no guarantee exists that the defendant will receive an advantageous judgment even if he or she cooperates with the prosecution.

In cases where a crime is spread out over a wide area, like organized crime activity, cooperation from the defendant leads to the prosecution of other major criminals. In such a case, the prosecution pleads for extenuating circumstances to be considered in court.

There are many cases of legal bargaining. In one trial in which a New York mafia boss was sentenced to life imprisonment, a murderer who had cooperated with the investigation was released after only a short incarceration.

Q Is there capital punishment in the USA?

Some states permit capital punishment, and others do

そうでない州とがあり、執行の方法も州によって異なります。2015年時点で死刑制度のない州はワシントンD.C.を含めて19州、またグアムやプエルトリコといったアメリカの植民地（信託統治領）の多くも死刑制度を廃止しています。

　凶悪な犯罪に悩むアメリカでは、死刑の是非は常に政治論争の主要なテーマとなっています。また州法ではなく、連邦政府の法律で裁かれる事件の犯人（連邦政府の施設や金融機関に対する犯罪や、広域組織犯罪等）にも死刑制度は適用されています。

　2016年の死刑囚の数は2,905人です。

アメリカの内政

Q　アメリカの国家予算の規模と収支の現状はどのようになっているのですか？

　アメリカはここ数年間にわたって、国家予算の収支を均衡させ、慢性的な財政赤字から抜け出そうと様々な政策を実行しています。ただ、こうした中、どの予算を削減し、かつ国民へのサービスをどのように実施して行くかということについては大統領と議会の意見が必ずしも一致せず、議論

not. As of 2015, there are nineteen states without capital punishment, including Washington, D.C. Many US trust territories such as Guam or Puerto Rico have also abolished the death penalty.

The rights or wrongs of the death penalty are always a major theme in political debates in the USA, where some atrocious crimes are committed. Capital punishment also applies to criminals tried under federal law (crimes against federal government facilities or financial organizations, crimes carried out over a wide area, etc.).

The number of prisoners on death row in 2016 totaled 2,905.

Domestic Affairs

Q What is the size, total revenue, and expenditure of the current US federal budget?

The US government has put various policies into effect in an attempt to reduce the chronic budget deficit. In the process of balancing expenditures and revenues over the past several years, the president and Congress have not always seen eye to eye. Frequent arguements arise over what should be reduced in the budget, and

の的となっています。

　共和党議員の反対にあうものの、2010年、オバマ政権は国民保険法案を通過させました。また2008年の経済危機からアメリカを立ち直させるための刺激策も成立させます。こうして政府支出が増加したことを受け、議会の共和党議員たちは、オバマ大統領の任期中の多くの時間を、政府支出削減のために費やさせたのです。

　2011年の政府予算はおよそ2兆1,700億ドルで、支出は3兆8,200億ドルと予想されていました。1兆6,500億ドルの赤字です。2001年にクリントン政権を引き継いだジョージ・W・ブッシュ以来、赤字は増え続けていたのです。この国家予算赤字は高止まりのまま今も続いているのです。

Q　アメリカはどのような警察制度を持っていますか？

　アメリカはそれぞれの自治体ごとに別個の警察組織があり、その地域の法律に従って行動します。それに対して、広域犯罪や金融関係に関する犯罪、さらに連邦政府に対する犯罪を捜査するために、地域の壁を超えて活動できるFBI、すなわち連邦警察があるのです。FBIは時には地方の警察と共同して事件の捜査にあたります。また、連邦政府にはFBIの他にも連邦麻薬捜査局（DEA）などもあって、広域麻薬犯罪に対して独自の捜査を展

how to put programs into effect.

Although Congressional Republicans opposed the plan, the Obama administration passed a policy for federal healthcare in 2010. The administration also enacted a "stimulus" plan to help the nation recover from the economic crash of 2008. As a result of these heavy federal expenditures, Republicans in Congress have devoted much of the duration of the Obama presidency to "cut federal spending."

In the 2011 federal budget, total revenue was estimated at $2.17 trillion and total estimated expenditures were $3.82 trillion, with a $1.65 trillion deficit. The deficit has been increasing since 2001 when George W. Bush took over from the Clinton administration. The current federal deficit remains at a record high.

Q What kind of police system exists in the USA?

A separate police force exists in each and every state, and the force acts in accordance with that state's laws. The FBI (the Federal Bureau of Investigation—in essence, the federal police), acts above and beyond regional boundaries in the investigation of widespread crimes, finance-related crimes, and crimes against the federal government. The FBI also cooperates with local police in their investigations. Other federal organizations, such as the DEA (Drug Enforcement

開しています。

Q アメリカの税制の特徴はどのようなものですか？

　毎年4月15日は、その前年の個人の確定申告の提出期限です。アメリカではたとえ会社に勤めていても、源泉徴収とは別に個人の収入をまとめて申告をしなければなりません。申告の種類はその人が住んでいる町と州、そして国の3種類です。

　皆この時期になると、いかに節税をするかということを考え、経理士と相談し、申告書をまとめあげます。個人の支出のどこまでがビジネスの経費とされるか、あるいは出張で長期その町を離れていたために、地方税が控除されるべきだとか、法に照らして考えるのです。

　アメリカの税金は日本と同じように直接税と間接税とに別れますが、間接税は州や地方によってかなり異なります。例えば、ニューヨーク市の消費税は8.875％ですが、隣のニュージャージーに行けば税率が7％と下がるため、大きな買い物をするときは、ニュージャージーまでドライブしていく人も多くいます。

Administration), play their own part in the investigation of widespread drug crimes.

Q What are the characteristics of the American tax system?

April 15th is the last date for taxpayers to file tax returns for the previous year's income. In the USA, company workers have to file income taxes even if tax has been withdrawn at the source. There are three kinds of forms to file: city, state, and federal.

As filing day draws near, people consider how they can pay fewer taxes, and they get the advice of accountants as they fill out their tax-return forms. They try to work out how they can account for personal expenses as business expenses, or whether they might be exempt from paying local taxes since they were away on business trips.

Taxes are divided into direct taxes and indirect taxes, just as in Japan. Indirect taxes differ considerably from state to state. For example, the sales tax (an indirect tax) of New York City is 8.875%, while New Jersey's is 7%—so some people from New York drive to this neighboring state for their large purchases.

Q アメリカの教育制度は日本とどのように違うのですか？

アメリカの教育制度が日本ともっとも違うところは、地方主導型の教育を実施しているということでしょう。学校で教えるカリキュラムも教科の内容も、学校の予算も全国均一ではなく、それぞれのローカル・コミュニティが主体となって決定します。学校に子供を通わせる親や地域の人々が、連邦政府よりもはるかにその地区の教育に影響力をもっているのです。

従って、教育の内容も質も、地方によってまちまちで、例えば、キリスト教の影響が強いコミュニティでは、社会科（あるいは生物）の授業でもダーウィンの進化論を教えない場所があるなど、子供がどこの地域のどのコミュニティに育ったかによって、受ける教育が異なってきます。ですから経済的に余裕のある親は、よりよい学校のある地区に引っ越したり、私立学校に子供を入れたりといった現象も目立つのです。

一方、アメリカの教育の良いところは、まず、全国均一のお定まりの教育ではなく、それぞれの地域の人が自分たちの子供の教育について真剣に参加できる環境があるということではないでしょうか。

アメリカでは地方によって多少差はありますが、6歳になると小学校に入ります。新学期は9月（と

Q How does the US educational system differ from the Japanese system?

The biggest difference between the US and Japanese educational systems is that most US education is administered by the states. The local community plays a major role in deciding the school curriculum, textbooks, teaching materials, and the budget, which are not allocated at a set national average. The parents of children who attend schools and residents of the city or state have a bigger say over local education than the federal government.

The content and quality of education therefore vary from region to region. The education children receive also varies according to the type of community they belong to. For example, in some Christian communities, Darwin's theory of evolution is not taught in social studies or biology. Wealthier parents sometimes move to regions with better schools, or send their children to private school.

One strength of the US educational system is that people can participate actively in deciding the education they want for their children rather than simply accepting a curriculum that has been decided for them by the government.

Children generally start attending school at the age of six, though this varies by region. The school year

ころによっては8月か10月）で、あとは日本と同
じように、中学・高校と合計で12年間教育を受け、
大学に入学します。たいていは小学校、中学校、
高校で12年間通いますが、地方によって多少異な
るようです。

アメリカの福祉と健康

Q アメリカ人にとって、何が大きな死因となっていますか?

　政府の統計によれば、アメリカ人の死因で圧倒
的に多いのが心臓疾患です。第2位が癌、次が車
の事故死となります。アメリカ人の平均寿命は
76.0歳、幼児の死亡率は1,000人あたり6.7人となっ
ています。

　アメリカでは、白人系以外、すなわちマイノリ
ティの1歳以下の乳幼児の死亡率が、白人系の同
年齢の死亡率の1.5倍であることなど、社会的な弱
者や低所得者、あらたに移民してきた家族の健康
問題がクローズアップされてきています。こうし
た人々の間ではその他に結核やエイズも広がりつ
つあり、貧富の差、人種の差と健康の問題をどう
解決するかが課題になっています。

begins in September (in some regions, in August or October). As in Japan, children attend elementary, junior high, and high schools for twelve years, and then some go on to college. Usually, they attend school for twelve years, but again, this number varies.

Welfare and Health

Q What is the major cause of death among Americans?

According to statistics, the overwhelming cause of death among Americans is heart disease. The second cause is cancer, and next is car accidents. Average life expectancy is 76 years; the infant mortality rate is 6.7 out of 1,000.

Health problems among socially disadvantaged groups, low-income people, or new immigrants are a source of concern. The infant mortality rate of non-white minorities is 1.5 times higher than that among the white population. Tuberculosis and AIDS are also spreading among minority groups. One challenge America faces is how to solve the economic-based issues of race and health.

Q アメリカの健康保険制度はどのようになっているのでしょうか？

　2008年時、アメリカでは人口の約16％の人が無保険の状態だといわれていました。これはアメリカに国民健康保険制度がなく、法人や個人がそれぞれ保険会社と契約する形で保険に加入しなければならなかったからです。従って、失業した場合、あるいはパートタイムなど、会社に正式に雇用されていない場合、または個人の病歴や疾病の実情などによって保険料金が高くなったりして、保険に加入できないまま生活をしているケースが多くあったのです。

　しかし、2010年には抜本的な健康保険改革が議会に提出され、オバマ政権のもと法案は通過したのです。この改革では、すべてのアメリカ国民が健康保険に入れるようにすることと、一方で健康保険料を低く抑えるという法令も含まれていました。

　アメリカにも国がカバーする保険システムがあります。高齢者用のメディケイドと低所得者向けのメディケアの2つです。連邦政府の赤字が増加している今、このシステムが現在の形のままで維持されるかどうか、疑問を投げかける人もいます。

Q What kind of health insurance system does the USA have?

As of 2008, almost 16 percent of Americans were reported not to be covered by health insurance. That is because no national health insurance system existed in the USA. Most people had been covered by the insurance that their employer or they themselves bought. However, this was costly for people who are unemployed, or for non-contractual workers such as part-timers. Moreover, for those who have experienced past illnesses or medical conditions, insurance premiums were quite high. The fact is that many people simply could not afford health insurance.

However, sweeping health care reforms were proposed and passed by the Obama administration in 2010. These reforms mandate all US citizens to have health insurance, while also enacting regulations to keep the cost of health insurance down.

National systems in which the federal government covers medical expenses do exist, such as Medicaid for seniors and Medicare for low-income people. With the federal deficit increasing, however, there is some question as to whether these systems will continue in their present form.

アメリカの外交

Q アメリカの孤立主義とはどのような考え方ですか？

　独立戦争とその後の経緯をみればおわかりのように、アメリカはもともとはヨーロッパの専制政治や束縛から自らを解き放つために、人々が団結して造られた国家です。

　こうしたことから、当然外国で起きた事に対して国家として強く干渉することに世論の上で大きな抵抗があったことは否めません。まして、独立国家として一歩一歩国家の体制を整えていったアメリカは、極力ヨーロッパ諸国のいざこざから自らを守ろうと、海外との非同盟の原則を貫いていったのです。

　特に1817年に大統領となったモンローは、この政策を強調したために、アメリカの孤立主義は、その後モンロー主義といわれるようになりました。

　アメリカが孤立主義の立場を本格的に放棄したのは、日本の真珠湾攻撃でした。それまでは、ヒトラーによるヨーロッパの動乱に対しても、イギリスやフランスに同情しながらも消極的な立場を貫いていたアメリカが、日本の攻撃で第2次世界大戦に突入し、その後も国際政治に主導的な立場をとるようになったのです。

　孤立主義の伝統は今でもアメリカに残っていま

第5代大統領ジェームズ・モンローが提唱したことにより、「モンロー主義」といわれる

American Diplomacy

Q What is US isolationism?

As the War of Independence and subsequent historical developments demonstrate, the USA was a nation created by people who united in a common desire to be free of the tyranny of European governments.

Not surprisingly, US public opinion shows great opposition to any national intervention in the affairs of foreign countries. America became an independent nation only by their own great efforts, one step at a time, and as a result there is a perception that America should keep well away from European disputes. This idea runs through their policies of non-alliance.

President Monroe emphasized a policy of isolationism in 1817. It was later called the Monroe Doctrine after him.

The USA officially abandoned isolationism after the Japanese attacked Pearl Harbor. Until then, the USA had been sympathetic to England and France in World War II, but the USA had remained on the sidelines. The Japanese attack brought the USA rushing into war, and thereafter it took a leading role in the international arena.

A certain tradition of isolationism still remains

す。特にベトナム戦争での失敗は、アメリカが海外の出来事に介入することの愚かさを国民に印象づけ、従来の「素晴らしいアメリカ」を維持するためにも、海外とは距離をおこうという動きが議会の中でも議論されました。

　孤立主義とは単なる外交戦略だけではなく、アメリカという国家の価値を守ろうとする、庶民のレベルから政治理念にまでいたる、1つのナショナリズムの現れでもあるのです。

Q 冷戦後のアメリカ外交にはどのような変化がありましたか？

　冷戦の終結によって、アメリカはソ連という強力なライバルを失いました。しかし、世界は冷戦構造がなくなったことによって、かえって複雑になり、地域紛争が激化する可能性が大きくなっているというのが、アメリカ政府の大方の見解といえそうです。ですから、例えば中東の和平や、ロシアの安定に積極的に貢献し、アメリカのプレゼンスを維持し、世界の安定に指導的な役割を果たしていこうというのが、現在のアメリカの外交政策であるといえましょう。

　アジアでは中国との関係をどう維持していくかというのが、アメリカにとって最大の課題となっています。また、発展を続ける東南アジア地域と

however. The failure of the Vietnam War impressed upon the American public the stupidity of overseas intervention, and voices were heard in Congress arguing that the country should maintain its distance from other countries to "keep America great."

Isolationism is not simply a diplomatic policy: it is also an expression of a certain type of generalized nationalism that reaches down to the general public. This is a nationalism that believes in the protection of America as a nation.

Q In what ways did US diplomacy change after the end of the Cold War?

With the end of the Cold War, the USA lost its more powerful rival, the Soviet Union. But in fact as a result the world has become an even more complicated place, and the possibility of regional disputes only the more likely. This seems to be the view of most people in the American government. Current US diplomatic policy, therefore, seems to consist of taking a leading role in global stabilization: for example, the USA helped bring about peace talks in the Mideast, and sought to make positive efforts toward stabilizing the situation in Russia.

The biggest issue that concerns American policy in Asia is how the USA will pursue its relations with China. Other international issues that the USA deals

の経済問題や、朝鮮半島の安定などに今後もアメリカはどんどん影響力を行使していくはずです。

Q アメリカの「人権外交」とはどのような外交のことですか？

　カーター大統領の時代から、アメリカの外交政策の基軸となってきたのが、人権外交です。民主主義を国是とするアメリカが、人権を侵害している国家に対して、経済制裁や政治的圧力をかけ、民主主義を守り、世界の安定を促進しようというのがその政策の骨子です。こうした外交の背景には、冷戦時代にはソ連に対する牽制、冷戦後ではアメリカそのものの影響力を正当化するためのPRの意味があることは否めません。

　確かに、アメリカの人権外交は世界で不当な差別や抑圧に苦しむ人々の政治的な拠り所となったことも多々ありましたし、それなりに評価できる成果もあげてきました。しかし、こうした外交政策がいわゆる「おせっかい」ととられ、相手を逆に硬化させたり、アメリカとの関係が悪化したりといった事態も招いています。その代表的な例が、天安門事件以来ぎくしゃくしてきた中国との関係でしょう。

　人権外交は、いわゆるアメリカの理想を掲げた外交政策です。しかし、世界が多様化していく中

with are problems arising from economic development in various countries in Southeast Asia, and the stability of the Korean Peninsula.

Q What is "human rights diplomacy"?

Human rights diplomacy became the principle axis of US diplomacy under President Carter. The key idea was that the USA, a nation with democracy as a national policy, applies economic sanctions or diplomatic pressure to any nation violating human rights. This was done in order to defend democracy and to promote global stability. Admittedly, behind such diplomacy lay a US intention to curb the power of the Soviet Union during the Cold War, and to justify and publicize America's power after the Cold War.

Actually, American human rights diplomacy became a political rallying point for all sorts of people suffering unjust discrimination and oppression around the world. It has shown demonstrable results. But such diplomacy can be taken as "meddlesome," and sometimes the other country simply becomes more stubborn and relations grow worse. The awkward relations the USA had with China after the Tiananmen Square massacre is one such example.

Human rights diplomacy supports an American ideal. But the world is diverse, and it is getting more

で、同じ人権そのものをみても様々な価値があり、戦後の一時期のように、アメリカが「世界の警察官」ではありえなくなった現実が、こうした外交政策の向こうに立ちはだかっているのも事実です。また、人権外交を進めるアメリカの中で、死刑制度が拡大し、貧困や抑圧から逃れてくる移民への入国制限が強化されるなどといった矛盾も見逃せません。

アメリカの「人権外交」は、アメリカの理想とプライドに支えられながらも、実際は世界の現実との中で外交的な駆け引きの道具としても利用されている、議論多き外交政策といえそうです。

Q アメリカと国連とはどのような関係にありますか？

ニューヨークにある国連の本部

アメリカはイギリスやソ連と共に国際連合の設立に大きな役割を果たしました。特に1941年にイギリスの首相ウインストン・チャーチルとフランクリン・ルーズベルト大統領とが発表した大西洋憲章が国連設立の主旨となり、1945年のサンフランシスコ会議で国連憲章の骨子が作成されました。

そして、国連の成立と共に、アメリカはフランス、イギリス、中国(当時は中華民国)、ソ連と共に、国連の常任理事国となりました。その後、冷戦の

so. Many different views exist about the issue of human rights alone. It is no longer practically viable for the USA to be the "global policeman" it was during the period after WWII. Moreover, one cannot ignore the contradiction in the American position: even while it advocates human rights abroad, the death penalty exists in most states, and stronger restrictions are being imposed on the number of immigrants fleeing poverty and oppression and entering US borders.

Even though it is underpinned by American ideals and pride, American human rights diplomacy was often actually used as a bargaining tool in foreign relations, so it has been a policy surrounded by much controversy.

Q What is the relationship of the USA with the UN?

Together with England and the Soviet Union, the USA played a major role in founding the United Nations. The Atlantic Charter announced by British Prime Minister Winston Churchill and American President Franklin D. Roosevelt in 1941 became the founding spirit of the United Nations. This was developed into the UN Charter at the UN Conference in San Francisco in 1945.

When the UN was established, the USA became a permanent member, along with France, England, China (then the "Republic of China"), and the Soviet Union.

進行と共に、アメリカは自由主義国の利益代表として、国連を国際政治の駆け引きの重要な舞台として利用し、イニシアチブをとってきたことは周知の事実です。

現在、冷戦の終結と共に、第2次世界大戦後の国際政治の中で設立され、強化された国連の在り方自体が問い直されています。アメリカも以前のように単に共産主義陣営を念頭に置いた国連への関わり方から、より混沌とした国際情勢の中でいかにアメリカの利益を国連の中で維持していくか試行錯誤を繰り返しています。

Q　アメリカの対日外交はどのように変化してきましたか？

戦後アメリカは日本をどのように自由主義陣営に組み込むかということを対日外交の中心に据えていました。従って、軍事面では日米安全保障条約を締結し、経済面では戦争で荒廃した日本経済の立て直しに積極的に協力し、日本を極東での戦略の要として位置付けていったのです。

しかし、日本が高度成長を遂げ、経済大国として繁栄すると、日本経済そのものがアメリカにとっても脅威となり、アメリカは日本に対して、今までは大目に見ていた日米間の経済上の様々な不公平を取り除こうと外交方針を大きく転換させます。また、軍事面でも日本に経済力相応の責任分担を要求するようになりました。

As the Cold War advanced, the USA took the initiative as a representative of the interest of free nations in using the UN as an important negotiation arena in international politics.

With the end of the Cold War, the whole purpose and existence of the UN, which after all was founded in the aftermath of WWII, has come into question. The USA is no longer concerned first and foremost with how to deal with the Communist bloc: it is now attempting to figure out how to further US interests in the UN given the more complicated international situation.

Q How has US diplomacy with Japan changed?

After WWII, the key point of US diplomacy with Japan was how best to incorporate Japan into the group of free nations. The USA concluded the US-Japan Security Treaty, helped build the Japanese economy after the devastation of war and set Japan up as a strategic point in the Far East.

As Japan achieved high economic growth and prospered, however, the Japanese economy became a threat. As a result, the USA made drastic changes in its diplomatic policy toward Japan. They tried to remove various unfair elements previously overlooked in the two countries' economies. The USA also began to ask Japan to take responsibility in the area of the military,

もう戦後の時代は終わりました。そして冷戦も終結し、アメリカの対日外交は新しい局面を迎えているといえそうです。アメリカにとって北朝鮮があり、中国の脅威は未だにあるとはいえ、21世紀の重要な外交相手として中国とは積極的に関係の改善を求めています。

こうした中で、日本とアメリカが世界経済の安定のための重要なパートナーとなりうるのか、あるいはアメリカのライバルとして外交の力をもって対抗していかなければならないのか課題は山積しています。時代の変化を考えると、今後の日米関係を予測するのはとても難しいといえそうです。

Q アメリカ同時多発テロ（9/11）はアメリカにどのような影響を与えましたか？

1971年当時、建設中のツインタワー

2001年の9月11日、民間航空機がハイジャックされ、ニューヨークのワールド・トレード・センター、ワシントンD.C.郊外にある国防総省のビル、ペンタゴンに墜落しました。およそ3,000人がこの事件で命を落としたのです。

このテロリストによる事件が、アメリカの歴史を変えるターニングポイントとなりました。まず最初の教訓は、アメリカがどれだけテロリズムに対して無防備であったかということです。攻撃の

in proportion to its economic power.

The post-war era is now over, and so is the Cold War. US diplomacy with Japan seems to have entered a new phase. Though North Korean issues remains unresolved, and the threat from China still exists, the USA has been working toward improving relations with China, which will be an important player in twenty-first-century diplomacy.

Under such circumstances, many questions surround Japan's relationship with the USA. Will it be possible for the two countries to cooperate as major partners working to ensure global stability? Or will Japan have to confront the USA as a rival? Predicting the future of Japan-U.S. relations is quite difficult in changing times.

Q What effect did 9/11 have on America?

On September 11, 2001, hijacked civilian aircraft crashed into the World Trade Center in New York and the Pentagon, the Department of Defense's building on the outskirts of Washington, D.C. Nearly 3,000 people were killed in the attacks.

This multiple terrorist incident was a turning point in American history. First of all, it was a lesson in how defenseless America is to terrorism. After the attack, all the airports and important institutions in America

後、アメリカは国中の空港や国の重要機関などで、セキュリティの尺度を高めざるをえませんでした。

加えて、アメリカ国民は保守的になり、テロ事件を起こしたテロリストが所属していたイスラム過激派を憎み、恐れるようになりました。この憎しみや恐れがイスラム教を信じる人への差別を誘発し、長きにわたってアメリカが維持してきた多様性を受け入れる精神を脅かすようになったのです。

同時に、ブッシュ政権は「テロへの戦い」を布告し、世界中で反アメリカを名乗る組織や政府に対して措置を講じ始めるのです。テロリスト集団を援助していたという理由で、アメリカはアフガニスタンに侵攻し、タリバン政権を壊滅させました。

次にアメリカはイラクに侵攻することを決定しました。反米グループをサポートしていたということで、サダム・フセイン政権を打倒するためです。

アメリカの象徴でもあったワールド・トレード・センター

こうした一連のアメリカの行動は、アメリカに対する反発を招きました。テロリストたちを取り締まることで、多くのイスラム教徒の心に憎しみを呼び起こしてしまったのです。世界中、特に中東ではこうした双方の緊張関係が高まっているのです。

ワールド・トレード・センターは、単なるニューヨークの象徴ではありません。アメリカという国自体の象徴なのです。空に高くそびえる2つのビ

had to tighten their security measures.

In addition, public opinion moved to the right, and the American public began to hate and fear the radical Islamic sect that the terrorists belonged to. This hate and fear became discrimination toward all believers in Islam, and threatened the democratic acceptance of diversity that America had promoted for many years.

At the same time, the Bush Administration declared the "War on Terror" and began to take action against anti-American organizations and governments around the world. Afghanistan was invaded because it supported terrorist groups, and the Taliban regime, which controlled it, was destroyed.

Furthermore, America decided to invade Iraq and destroy the regime of Saddam Hussein because of its support for anti-American groups.

These actions created a backlash against America, and the anti-terrorist measures awoke hatred in the hearts of many Muslims. Throughout the world, and in the Middle East in particular, this situation caused great tension.

The World Trade Center was a symbol not just of New York, but of America itself. The image of the destruction of these two soaring towers was so

ルが破壊された場面はあまりにも衝撃的で、事件後、メディアによっては特定の場面を放映しないこともありました。多くの人が、多様性を受け入れるというアメリカの美徳が、建物の崩壊とともにくだかれてしまったと言っています。

　アメリカには、民主的な自由は世界中に広まるべきだという考え方があります。この信念が同時多発事件以降、さらに強くなっていったのです。

　アメリカは日本を含めた海外の同盟国に、軍事的援助を求めています。新しい軍事秩序がテロに対抗するという名目で構築されようとしています。日本も同調することを突きつけられているのです。こうした点からも、9/11はアメリカだけの影響にとどまらず、世界を巻き込むことになったといえそうです。

アメリカの軍事と宇宙開発

Q　アメリカは今でも軍事に力を入れているのですか？

　1990年代、財政赤字削減の一環として、アメリカの連邦政府は、アメリカ国内の軍事基地を閉鎖す

shocking that after the attacks, the media refrained from showing certain scenes of their destruction. Many people say that America's democratic virtue of freely accepting diverse cultures was destroyed along with the World Trade Center.

There is a belief in America that democratic freedom should be spread around the world. This belief became much stronger after 9/11.

America requested military aid from its allies abroad, including Japan. A new military order was established in the name of fighting terrorism, and Japan was thrust into joining it. From that perspective, 9/11 was an event that had an important influence not just on America, but on the world as well.

American Military and Space Development

Q Does the USA still place an emphasis on the military?

In the 1990s, as a part of the deficit reduction, the federal government made efforts to reduce military

るなど、軍事費の削減に取り組みました。その結果、1989年に3,036億ドルだった軍事支出が、95年には2,719億ドル弱にまで削減されました。

とはいえ、21世紀に入り、軍事費は再び増え、2010年の時点で、アメリカ政府は国防総省、軍事研究開発費、海外オペレーションに6,638億ドルを費やしました。

ただし、そうした中でも、アメリカが世界の安定に影響を与えるリーダーであるべきだという意識は未だに強く、軍事費を削減する中で、いかに自らのプレゼンスを保っていくかという課題に連邦政府は取り組んでいます。しかし、アメリカは国連での平和維持軍に対する支出も抑制しており、今後は軍事戦略より外交戦略による国際政治への参加が増えていくのではと思われます。とはいえ、アフガニスタンやイラクに比べて、シリアへの地上軍の投入は少ないとはいえ、アメリカ軍の介入は続いてきたのです。

Q CIAはアメリカではどのように評価されているのですか？

1994年5月にオルドリッチ・エイムズというCIAの職員が、9年間にわたってソ連にアメリカの情報を売っていたという事件が発覚しました。彼が売っていた情報は、アメリカのために働いて

expenditures. The government closed down military bases in the US. Military spending was $303.6 billion in 1989, but it was reduced to $271.9 billion in 1995.

However, in the twenty-first century, military spending is back on the rise. In 2010, the US government spent $663.8 billion on the Department of Defense, military research and development, and overseas operations.

The consciousness of the USA's leadership role in global stability is strongly alive. However, with a staggering federal deficit, the government is struggling with the issue of maintaining American presence while also making cuts in military expenditure. The USA restricted its contribution to the UN PKO for a while, so it looked as if diplomatic rather than military strategy would emerge as the most important feature of its international politics, yet U.S. military involvement—in Afghanistan, Iraq, and in a less "boots on the ground" manner in Syria—has continued.

Q How is the CIA thought of in the USA?

In May 1994, federal prosecutors accused CIA agent Aldrich H. Ames of having sold state secrets to the Soviet Union over a period of nine years. The information he sold was highly important, including a list

CIA=Central Intelligence Agency
政府直属の組織で、中央情報局のこと。アメリカの外交や国防政策に必要な諜報活動を行う

いたソ連や東欧のスパイのリストなど、大変貴重なもので、そのためにアメリカ側のスパイ網は軒並み破壊され、ソ連ではアメリカに情報を売っていた人物が最低でも10人は処刑されたのではといわれています。

こうしたスキャンダルのせいで、CIAはソ連が崩壊し、冷戦が終結するという世界史の上でも重大な出来事を充分に予測できなかったのです。

その結果、CIAの存在価値そのものを疑う声が議会の中でも盛り上がり、冷戦の終結とともに、はたして昔のようにCIAが必要なのだろうかという疑問が提示されたのです。これに対して、CIA側は、まだ世界は安定していないと主張し、その存在価値を強調しています。また、CIAは否定していますが、CIAが組織の生き残りのために日本をはじめとする経済上のライバルに対しての経済諜報活動をはじめているといううわさも流れています。

さらに最近では、2013年にCIAの元局員、エドワード・スノーデンが暴露した内容が物議を醸しました。情報機関とともにアメリカ国家安全保障局（NSA）が情報収集する際に使う世界規模のネットワークや手口を告発したのです。これによりアメリカ国内だけでなく海外の安全保障に関わる組織でも、法の枠を超えた取り組みを論議することになり、これからもこの論争は続くものと思われます。

of Soviet and Eastern European spies working for the USA. The espionage network on the US side was left in ruins. On the Soviet side, at least ten spies selling information to the USA were reportedly executed.

In the midst of this scandal, the CIA was unable to prepare itself for a very important development in world affairs—the collapse of the Soviet Union and the end of the Cold War.

Those incidents fostered suspicion about the whole purpose and existence of the CIA, and a debate was held in Congress as to whether the CIA was still relevant to the modern world. The CIA argues that the world is not yet stable, so there was still a reason for its being. Although the CIA itself denies them, there are reports that the USA had even started economic espionage on its rivals, including Japan, to ensure its survival.

More recently, the controversial revelations in 2013 by former CIA employee Edward Snowden showed a global network of National Security Agency (NSA) information gathering, in combination with other U.S. intelligence agencies. This led to debate over the extra-legal efforts overseas and within the U.S. of these security-related organizations, leading to a controversy that still continues.

Q アメリカの宇宙開発の将来はどのようになるでしょうか？

NASAのマーク

　アメリカは数年にわたって、国家予算を立て直すため、宇宙開発の予算にも厳しい枠が設けられています。しかし、2010年までにNASAの予算は187億ドルになっていました。そうした中、NASAでは、宇宙開発を進めていこうと様々な工夫をしています。大型打ち上げロケットの完成が目前に迫っています。オリオンという宇宙船で、国際宇宙ステーションと共同して、最新のテクノロジーを駆使し開発しています。

　この前提に立って、太陽系、特に火星の探査に力を注いでいます。21世紀中には火星に人間が旅立つかもしれません。2010年には議案が通り、2030年代までに有人火星探査を実現するとしたのです。NASAは、宇宙開発に向けてロシア、ヨーロッパ、日本と協力して宇宙ステーションを建設した後、日本を含めた各国といっしょに、アメリカからも宇宙飛行士を送っています。

Q What is the future of US space development?

Although for several years the US government set a strict ceiling on the space development budget in its commitment to reduce the national budget, by 2010 the budget for NASA had returned to $18.7 billion. But NASA is still managing to promote space development. It is near completion of a new heavy lift rocket program, is developing a new space-travel capsule named Orion, and it is in active cooperation with the International Space Station in a multinational effort to reflect new, modern technologies.

As far as development is concerned, NASA is concentrating its efforts on probing the solar system, particularly Mars. It is possible that human beings might journey to Mars in the twenty-first century. In 2010, a US bill was signed allowing for a manned Mars mission by the 2030s. NASA, after constructing a space station with Russia, Europe, and Japan as a base for space development, has been sending American astronauts into space alongside those from other nations, including Japan.

◆コラム◆　ドナルド・トランプが大統領に選ばれて

　2016年のアメリカ大統領選挙は、アメリカに深い傷を残した選挙であったといわれています。

　当初メキシコや中東からの移民に対して厳しい姿勢をとり、人種差別主義者とまで批判されたドナルド・トランプ氏が大統領選挙で勝利したことは確かに多くの人に衝撃を与えました。

　アメリカには移民社会が生み出す独特の不平等感が根強くありました。それは、マイノリティと呼ばれるアフリカ系アメリカ人や中南米出身のアメリカ人と、元々アメリカ社会を牽引してきた白人系の人々との間にある不信感です。歴史的には差別を受けていた側はマイノリティの人々でした。従って、これらの人々に平等な機会を与えようと、アメリカ社会は様々な取り組みをしてきたのです。しかし格差社会が深刻になる中で、これらの取り組みのみに焦点が当てられたことで、白人系の人々、特に白人系の男性の間に、自分たちは取り残され、見捨てられているという疎外感が蔓延していったのです。この疎外感を意識した人々こそが、ドナルド・トランプに投票したのです。

　逆に、マイノリティの多くや、リベラル派の人々は、今回の選挙の結果を時代に逆行したものだとして、失望感と警戒感をあらわにします。人々の間にこうした深刻な分断がおきたことが、今回の大統領選挙が残した傷なのです。トランプ政権がこれからこの傷をどのように癒し、懸念される移民政策などに手をつけるのか、まだ見えない部分も多々あります。

　しかし、アメリカ人の中に生まれた人種や移民への考え方の相違からくる対立が、社会の中に今までにない相互不信を植え付けていることだけは事実です。アメリカは、将来の社会のあり方を大きく左右しかねない試練の時代をむかえつつあるのです。

Chapter 4

The US Economy

第4章 アメリカの経済活動

アメリカ経済の背景

Q ドルとはどのような貨幣ですか？

日本の円は日銀券といわれますが、ドルは連邦準備券といわれ、連邦準備銀行が発行し、管理しています。アメリカで中央銀行が通貨を発行管理し、金融政策を統括するようになったのは、なんと1913年のことで、以前は地方分権制度の原則の元、銀行の活動も半ば野放しの状態であったといわれています。辺境ではワイルドキャット・バンクと呼ばれる、信用取り引きもままならない金融機関が乱立し、独自の銀行券を発行したことで、しばしば金融危機を招いたりしたといわれています。

現在ドルは1ドル札から100ドル札までの6種類の紙幣が一般に流通し、補助貨幣として1セント（通称ペニー）、5セント（通称ニッケル）、10セント（通称ダイム）、25セント（通称クォータ）、50セント、さらに1ドルの硬貨も流通しています。ドルのことは俗に「バック」といわれ、日常会話では、2ドルのことを、2バックスなどと表現されることが多くあります。

Background of the US Economy

Q What kind of currency is the US dollar?

In the same way that the Japanese yen is officially referred to as a Bank of Japan note, the US dollar is officially called a Federal Reserve note—and it is issued and controlled by the Federal Reserve Bank. It was actually in 1913 that the central bank of the US began to issue and control currency and standardize its finance policies. Previous to that, banks were left almost entirely to their own devices under a decentralized system. The frontier was apparently overrun by financial institutions (nicknamed "wildcat banks") making chaotic credit transactions, issuing bank notes of their own and causing frequent financial crises.

US dollars are now distributed in six kinds of bills, in denominations from 1 to 100 dollars, with supplementary coins—1 cent (a penny), 5 cents (a nickel), 10 cents (a dime), 25 cents (a quarter), 50 cents (a half dollar) and 1 dollar. The slang name for a dollar is a "buck." Thus one often hears 2 dollars expressed as "2 bucks" in daily life.

Q ドルはいつごろから世界に流通するようになったのですか？

ニューヨークにある連邦準備銀行

　ニューヨークの連邦準備銀行の地下にある巨大な金庫には、世界各国が保有する金が保管され、国際間の債務の支払いが発生すると、その巨大な金庫の中で、ある国の金庫から別の国の金庫へと金が移動します。

　ここは、ドルへの高い信用に基づき、アメリカへ金が流入してきた頃のことを思い出させる場所として観光名所にもなっています。

　ドルが本格的に世界の機軸通貨となったのは、第2次世界大戦後にアメリカが世界一の債権国として活動するようになったときです。しかし、1960年代後半以降は、アメリカ経済の相対的な落ち込みもあり、ドルの信用は以前ほどはなくなり、実質的にはどんどん切り下げられていきます。そして世界の通貨相場は、変動相場制へと移行していきました。

　現在でも、ドルは世界の機軸通貨です。しかし、以前のように、全てをドルをもとに換算し、判断する時代ではなくなりました。ダイナミックな世界経済活動の中で、世界の貨幣の相場が相互に影響を与えあい、その結果にアメリカの金融界、そして経済界も一喜一憂しているのが現在の状況なのです。

Q When did the US dollar begin to have international distribution?

The huge safes underneath the New York Federal Reserve Bank store gold belonging to every country. Whenever a debt is paid by one country to another, the gold moves from one safe to another underground.

The Federal Reserve Bank is now a tourist spot too, a reminder of the time gold flowed into the USA based on the high value accorded the US dollar.

The US dollar became the key world currency when the USA became the world's largest creditor after WWII. In the latter half of the 1960s, however, the US economy declined, and the dollar was seen to have less value than before—and it was in fact devalued. World currency then shifted to a floating standard.

The US dollar is still a key world currency, but it is no longer the standard of all exchange and value. World currencies all affect each other in the current dynamic world markets, which is a source of mixed blessings as far as the US financial and business worlds are concerned.

Q アメリカ国内の経済活動にはどのような地域差があり ますか？

アメリカは州や地方によって所得や賃金、そし て経済力そのものにもかなりばらつきがあります。 しかも、アメリカには日本にとっての東京のよう な場所はなく、大企業の本社もその企業が創業し た場所でそのまま成長するので全米に分散するこ とになります。例えば、日用雑貨などを製造販売 する巨大企業プロクター・アンド・ギャンブルの 本社はオハイオ州のシンシナティ市ですし、自動 車産業の多くはデトロイトとその周辺に集中し、 コカ・コーラの本社はアトランタというふうに、 例を挙げればきりがありません。ただ、一般的に は金融関係やメディア関係はニューヨークに、製 造業や流通業はアメリカの真ん中、ミッドウエス トに、ハイテク関係は西海岸といった大まかな住 み分けはあるようです。

Q アメリカの貿易収支はどのように推移しているのです か？

アメリカは近年ずっと貿易収支の赤字に悩まさ れてきました。特に中国、メキシコ、日本、それ にドイツとの貿易赤字が目立っています。アメリ カの貿易収支が赤字になりはじめたのは1980年代 になってからのことでした。特に、80年代半ばに は、輸出の主力商品ともいえる自動車産業の不振

Q What regional differences exist in the US domestic economy?

Considerable differences in terms of income, wage, and economic power exist from state to state in the USA. No single center like Tokyo exists, and since most large enterprises develop where they were founded, companies tend to be scattered all over the country. Procter & Gamble, for example, a huge manufacturer of household goods and necessities, has its headquarters in Cincinnati, Ohio. Detroit and its environs have a large concentration of car manufacturers, and Coca-Cola's headquarters are in Atlanta. But generally speaking, financial business and the media are heavily concentrated in New York, manufacturers and distributors in the Midwest, and the high-tech industry on the West Coast.

Q What shifts have there been in the US trade balance?

The US has been troubled by a trade deficit for many years now. Recently, the deficit is most outstanding with China, Mexico, Japan, and Germany. The US trade balance turned to deficit in the 1980s—particularly the mid-'80s, when it exceeded $95 billion. This was exacerbated by the decline of the auto industry,

も手伝って、赤字幅は950億ドルを突破し、日本との貿易摩擦も深刻化しました。赤字幅は時により変動しつつも、減少傾向にあります。商務省によると、2011年の統計では482億ドルになっています。

　ただ、この統計をどのように読むかということになると色々な意見があります。通関ベースではなく送金ベースでのお金の流れや、入国者がアメリカに持ち込む資産、アメリカに進出した外資系企業がアメリカに投資したりアメリカから輸出している収入などを加えると、少なくとも日米間での国際収支はアメリカの黒字にすらなるのではないかという意見もあるのです。

Q　アメリカはどのようなものを輸出し、どのようなものを輸入しているのですか？

　アメリカの輸出の主力商品はコンピュータ通信機器、航空機やそれに関連する部品、自動車、工作機械、科学及び化学製品などで、その他農産物も主要な輸出商品です。それに対して輸入は輸出と同じく自動車や工業製品、コンピュータ通信機器、工作機械、鉄鋼及び金属製品、紙、化学製品、衣料品、石油製品などとなります。輸出の主力商品と同じ商品が輸入されていたり、輸出される商品を製造するための材料が輸入されていたりといった現状は、日々アメリカ経済が世界と一体化

which brought serious trade friction with Japan. But the deficit has fluctuated and has even declined. According to Department of Commerce statistics, the 2011 deficit was $48.2 billion.

Opinions vary about how to interpret these statistics. One opinion even has it that the US trade deficit, particularly that with Japan, is actually a surplus if one takes into consideration wire transaction, the money people bring into the US on their persons, the money Japanese companies in the US invest, and the revenues they attain from export.

Q What items does the US export and import?

Major US export items include computer telecommunication apparatuses, airplanes and related parts, cars, machine tools, scientific equipment, chemicals and agricultural products. Major import items include cars, industrial products, computer telecommunication apparatuses, machine tools, steel and metal products, paper, chemical products, clothing and petroleum products. The US thus imports many of the same sort of items as it exports. The fact that it imports materials to produce goods to be exported shows how bound up

しつつあることを如実に物語っています。

　いわゆる先進国型の加工貿易とは違い、原料も製品も共に輸出し輸入しているというのがアメリカの貿易の特徴ともいえそうです。

Q リーマン・ショックとは何ですか？

ニューヨークにあったリーマン・ブラザースの本社ビル

　アメリカでも最もよく知られた投資銀行の名前が、リーマン・ブラザースです。2008年にこの銀行が倒産すると、世界中の金融市場が混乱し、世界中で景気が下降線をたどりました。状況は悪化するばかりで、その状況から派生し、「大不況」と呼ばれています。

　2007年、低所得者向けの住宅ローンであるサブプライムローンが破綻し、銀行は負債を抱え続けることになります。90年代に日本で起きたバブル景気の崩壊と同じような危機的な状況でした。

　リーマン・ブラザースは、サブプライムローン危機により膨大な額の借金を背負ったのです。そしてそのまま倒産しました。

　パニック状態は2年続きました。さらに当時の投資先にも関係するギリシャ経済の崩壊により、リーマン・ショックの影響は拡大しました。

with the world economy the US economy is.

The fact that the US exports and imports both materials and products rather than just manufactured goods—which is the general pattern of advanced nations—is perhaps its most defining characteristic.

Q What is the Lehman Shock?

Lehman Brothers was one of America's most famous investment banks. When it went bankrupt in 2008, it affected financial markets around the world at a time when there was a world-wide recession, aggravating the situation dramatically, such that it spawned what came to be known as the "Great Recession."

In 2007, housing loans for low-income earners called "subprime loans" caused the amount of bad debt held by banks to increase, and there was an economic crisis similar to the bursting of Japan's economic bubble in the early '90s.

Lehman Brothers lost huge amounts of money because of all its bad debt resulting from subprime loans, and it went bankrupt.

This caused a panic that lasted almost two years, and things like the collapse of the Greek economy—closely related to the investment decisions of that period—have created even more instability and strengthened the Lehman Shock's effect.

まずは同時多発テロ事件後に株価が大幅に暴落しました。そしてITバブルの崩壊があり、さらにはリーマン・ショックへと続いたのです。世界を牽引する経済は大きく乱高下しました。当初オバマ政権は、2007‐8年に問題を起こした金融機関のリーダーを何人か採用したことで批判を受けましたが、リーマン・ショック後の様々な問題を乗り越えたことで信頼を回復し、2014年以降は景気も上向いたことから、失業率の改善にも寄与したのです。

Q　環境関連ビジネスの今後はどうなりますか？

　リーマン・ショックの後、政権をとったオバマは、環境関連のビジネスを手厚く保護するという重要な約束をしました。その一つが、自動車の需要を回復させることでした。不景気が続いた間、世界最大の自動車会社であったジェネラル・モーターズは倒産に追い込まれていました。すぐに日本のトヨタがリコールのスキャンダルや、2011年に起きた東日本大震災の影響で部品の調達が滞り、苦境に立たされました。いかにしてアメリカの自動車業界がこうした状況に対応するかは明確にはなっていません。日本のエコカーの技術は他国の技術に勝ると言われており、アメリカの車は

From the crash in stock prices after 9/11 to the collapse of the IT bubble to the Lehman Shock, the world's leading economy has had a very bumpy ride. Although initially criticized over his decision to employ some of the financial sector's leaders involved in the troubles of 2007–8, the Obama Administration has gotten credit for overcoming many of the worst results of the Lehman Shock, and the U.S. economy in the period from 2014 has experienced positive growth and a lowering of the unemployment figures seen after the Shock.

Q What will the future of environment-related businesses be?

When President Obama took office in the wake of the Lehman Shock, one of his important promises was to give support to environment-related businesses. One of his main tasks was restoring demand for automobiles during a recession which brought about the bankruptcy of the world's largest automaker, General Motors. Soon after, the important Japanese automaker Toyota began to struggle due to a recall scandal and supply-chain production problems related to the 2011 Tohoku Earthquake. How the American car industry will respond to this situation is not yet clear. Japanese technology for producing eco-friendly cars is said to be more advanced

それにどう対応するのか？　多くの疑問が残って
います。

　どのようにしてアメリカが環境保全技術、自然
エネルギーと向き合っていくかはとても大事なこ
とです。グローバルに競争していくためには、こ
れらの技術を可能にできるかどうかが大切になっ
ています。それは今も、これからもです。今まで、
アメリカは物質主義社会で、世界経済におけるスー
パーパワーでした。経済問題にも直結する地球温
暖化や他の自然環境に関する問題にどう取り組む
か。これは見逃すことのできない政治的な課題で
もあるのです。ところが、新トランプ政権は、環
境保全に関する「時計の針を戻そう」としている
かのようです。地球は温暖化していないといい、
環境にやさしいことよりも、経済的な成長のほう
が急務だと言っているのです。将来にわたるアメ
リカ経済の成長にとって、巨大市場であるアメリ
カにおいて環境関連ビジネスをどう育てるか、そ
して日本などの競争相手とどう競い合うかが大き
な影響を与えることになるでしょう。

than that of other countries, but how will the American car industry respond? Many questions remain.

It is very important to be able to predict how America will be able to compete in terms of green technology, energy, and production, and this ability will have a big impact on how well it can compete globally, now and in the future. Until now, America has been a materialistic society and the world's economic superpower. Dealing with global warming and other environmental problems that are presenting new economic challenges will be an important political issue that must be dealt with. In the meantime, the new Trump Administration appears intent on "turning the clock back" on environmental protections, not convinced that global warming has taken place, and arguing that economic growth is more important than ecologically-friendly measures. In the future, how environment-related businesses can predict the future of the giant American market and compete with competitors such as Japan will affect America's economic growth.

4
アメリカの経済活動
The US Economy

199

アメリカの産業界

Q アメリカの自動車業界が再生したと聞きますが、現在はどうなのですか？

1980年代、アメリカの自動車業界は日本やドイツをはじめとした外国からの自動車に押されて経営が悪化、何度もリストラを繰り返しました。燃費が悪く壊れやすいというのがアメリカ車に対する大方のイメージでした。

アメリカの自動車産業の礎を築いたヘンリー・フォード

自動車産業はあらゆる産業にリンクした基幹産業の1つです。従って、アメリカの自動車産業の停滞は、アメリカの産業界全体に様々な波紋を呼びおこしました。しかし、90年代に入って、アメリカの自動車業界は見事にカムバックしました。例えば、フォードの場合はピックアップと呼ばれる小型トラックや自家用車ではトーラスの成功などで、96年には330万台近くを販売し、ホンダなど早くからアメリカに進出してきた日本車業界にも脅威を与えました。

ただ、昨今では外国車が再び盛り返しをみせ、たとえば2008年におきた経済危機など、アメリカ自動車業界はまたしても影響を受けています。ガソリン価格の高騰、CO_2排出への顧客の意識の高まりなどもあり、米自動車業界の衰退を後押ししたのです。フォード、GM、クライスラーの米三

US Industries

Q What is the current situation of the US auto industry?

In the 1980s, the US auto industry declined, and many lay-offs occurred, as pressure was felt from the auto industry in Japan and Germany. The general opinion of American cars was that they had poor fuel efficiency and were continually breaking down.

The auto industry is a key one, a lifeline to all sorts of other industries. Its stagnation had a ripple effect all over the US industrial world. But the US auto industry made a wonderful comeback in the 1990s. Ford, for example, had great success with its pickup trucks and Taurus family cars, and in 1996 sold nearly 3.3 million cars. This boom posed a threat to Japanese auto manufacturers like Honda that had made such inroads in the US markets.

However, these days foreign cars are once again catching up, and the US auto industry was once again impacted, for instance, by the economic crash of 2008. Rising oil costs and a new consumer awareness of carbon footprints also contributed to the sharp decline of US car manufacturing. The "Big Three" of the

大自動車メーカーは、2008年には250億ドルの補助を政府に求めざるをえませんでした。政府は174億ドルを貸し付けたのです。

最近では、中国が自動車業界を大きく牽引しています。2010年には1,830万台の車が生産され、次が日本で960万台、続いてアメリカが第3位に甘んじて、770万台でした。

Q アメリカのコンピュータ産業の現状はどのようになっているのですか？

コンピュータ産業を牽引してきたIBMがパーソナルコンピュータを発売したのは1981年のことでした。以来、コンピュータ産業は着実に成長を続け、今やアメリカの経済を牽引する産業として注目を集めています。

特に、アメリカのコンピュータ業界は90年代に入って飛躍的に成長しました。インターネットの普及とパーソナルコンピュータの普及がその要因です。また、海外でのコンピュータ需要の増加も無視できません。コンピュータ・インダストリー・アルマナックの統計によれば、2008年、アメリカだけで2億6,400万台のコンピュータがあり、その数は飛躍的に伸び続けています。とくに、タブレットや初期のPCを超える機能をもつ機器の人気が上昇しているのです。

US automotive industry—Ford, General Motors, and Chrysler—had to request $25 billion in federal assistance to stay afloat in 2008. The federal government loaned them $17.4 billion.

Currently, China tops the list of global leaders in auto manufacturing, with 18.3 million cars produced in 2010. Japan follows with 9.6 million cars produced, and the US trails behind at third place with 7.7 million.

Q What is the current state of the US computer industry?

In 1981, IBM, a leader of the computer industry, introduced the personal computer, or PC. Since then, the computer industry has grown tremendously, and has become a dynamo of the US economy.

This industry showed particularly high growth in the 1990s with the proliferation of the Internet and PCs. There was also an increased demand for PCs overseas. According to Computer Industry Almanac statistics, 264.1 million personal computers were in use in the US in 2008. This number has continued to grow considerably, particularly as tablets and other devices with capabilities matching or surpassing earlier PCs have become increasingly popular.

2008年、コンピュータ業界の成長率は年間約3.8％といわれています。そして業界全体の売り上げは500億ドルを優に超えます。

　また、コンピュータ産業はあのマイクロソフト社の例でもおわかりのように、個人の才能次第で巨大企業に成長する夢のある産業ともいわれ、多くの起業家がどんどん成長しているのもこの業界の特徴です。他にも、目覚ましい躍進を遂げたグーグルやアップルなど、ここ10数年、この業界のトレンドは維持されています。

グーグル社の外観

Q　シリコンバレーとはどのようなところですか？

シリコンバレーにはアップル、グーグル、インテルなどの名だたる企業が集まっている

　シリコンバレーとはサンフランシスコの南側からサンノゼにいたる地域を指します。そこに、数えきれないハイテク産業のオフィスが集まっていることから、このニックネームがついたのです。シリコンバレーは、単にアメリカのコンピュータをはじめとしたハイテク産業を代表するだけではなく、そうした環境を求めて世界中から頭脳が集中する場所としても知られています。日本やヨーロッパからもさまざまな企業が進出し、この地域一帯がコンピュータ産業をリンクしたグローバル・ビレッジへと変化しています。

　起業家を育て、投資を呼び込むことで知られるシリコンバレーは、ひとつの会社が10以上のプロ

In 2008, the US computer industry generated $50.6 billion, showing a 3.8 percent annual growth rate.

The computer industry is said to be an industry where individual talent can give rise to huge enterprises and where dreams of success can indeed be realized—there is the famous example of Microsoft Corporation but the dramatic rise of Google, Apple, and others in recent decades shows this trend to be continuing. Indeed one noticeable feature of this industry is the prolific growth of many entrepreneurs.

Q What kind of place is Silicon Valley?

Silicon Valley is the nickname for the area stretching from South San Francisco to San Jose where a great many hi-tech companies are concentrated. It is famous not only for its hi-tech industry, but also as a place where the best and the brightest from all over the world have gathered in search of just such an environment. Many Japanese and European companies have also moved into this area, making it a computer-networked global village.

As an area known for nurturing entrepreneurs and attracting investment capital, the dynamics have been

ジェクトを同時に動かすなど、そのダイナミックさが特徴です。しかし、そのうちのいくつのプロジェクトが実現するかといえば、ほとんどが不成功なのです。数ある中のたった1つか2つが、世界規模の成功をつかむのです。

Q アメリカの宇宙産業の未来はどのようになるでしょうか?

NASA
1958年にアイゼンハワー大統領の署名により発足した政府機関

　アメリカの航空産業界は、現在こぞってNASAなどと協力し宇宙開発に乗り出しています。ボーイング社の例をとれば、民間航空機以外のマーケットの36%がアメリカ航空宇宙局のスペースプログラムによるもので、その割合は、空軍からの受注を大きく引き離しています。開発される分野は、単に経済的で性能の高い宇宙船の開発にとどまらず、宇宙の軍事利用、地球の環境保全や様々な開発事業、さらには通信ビジネスへの応用など、多岐に亘っているのです。21世紀の航空産業にとって、宇宙関連のビジネスの占める割合は、ますます大きくなっていきそうです。

Q アメリカの農業の現状はどのようになっているのですか?

　アメリカの農業は、農家1軒あたりの農地が日本の160倍以上ともいわれる広大な土地に大規模

interesting—a firm might invest in ten or more projects, but expects most to "not make it", and is hoping instead for one or two to be breakaway successes on the global stage.

Q What future trends can be foreseen in the US space industry?

The US aviation industry is collaborating in space development with NASA and others. For example, 36% of the orders for Boeing's non-commercial-flight craft market is for NASA's space program. This is much larger than the Air Force's order. Areas of development include designing economical and efficient spaceships, but attention will also be given to the military use of space, the protection of the earth's environment and other development projects, the application of space development technology to the telecommunications industry, and much else besides. Space-related business looks like it will continue to grow in the twenty-first century.

Q What is the current state of US agriculture?

The agricultural industry in the USA has developed over a vast farmland, in which a single farm can be as

農業生産額(2011年)世界シェア		
1位	中国	17.3%
2位	EU	7.4%
3位	インド	7.1%
4位	アメリカ	4.3%
5位	ブラジル	3.4%
8位	日本	1.9%

な機械や先進技術を導入して発展しました。

中には、そうした経営が成功し、食品マーケットに進出し、巨大な利益をあげた農業経営者も多くいます。例えば、アメリカ最大のジュースメーカーで世界にネットワークを拡張しているトロピカーナ・プロダクツを創業したアンソニー・ロッシも、30ドルをポケットに入れてイタリアからアメリカに移住してきた後、苦労の末フロリダで農業をはじめ、ジュース業界に進出し現在の巨大企業を造り上げたのです。

農業人口がどんどん減少している現在においても、アメリカの農業の規模はその耕作面積からみても旧ソ連を抜いて世界のトップの座を維持しています。

現在農産物はアメリカにとって重要な輸出品の1つです。小麦ととうもろこしの輸出額は合計で94億5,000万ドルと世界一、米の輸出額はタイに次いで世界第2位となっています。また肉の生産量は3,135万トンとこれも世界一のレベルです。

ただ、こうした農業にも、過剰投資による農家の倒産、肥料の投入のし過ぎや地下水の枯渇による耕作地の減少などといった深刻な問題があるのも事実です。また、今後も農業人口はどんどん減少していくことが予想され、アメリカの農業も先進国の農家が抱えるのと同じような問題を抱えているのです。

他にも見るべき点があります。ポジティブな面としては、農家が最新技術を使って収穫をチェッ

much as 160 times larger than one in Japan. Large-scale machinery and advanced technology are used.

Many farmers have made a lot of money by advancing into the manufactured food market. Anthony Rossi, who founded Tropicana Products, the largest American juice producer which is expanding all over the world, immigrated to the US from Italy with only $30 in his pocket. After many hardships, he started a farming business in Florida, then got into the juice industry and founded his huge company.

Despite the sharp decrease in the farming population now, the sheer scale of US agriculture makes it a world leader, surpassing even the Soviet Union.

Agricultural products are an important American export item. Total wheat and corn exports amount to $9.45 billion, the most in the world. Rice exports are second only to Thailand; total meat production is 31.35 million tons, also the most in the world.

But serious problems exist in agriculture: bankruptcy of farms due to excessive investment, and decrease of land for cultivation caused by over-application of fertilizer and drought. The farming population is expected to decrease. US agriculture thus faces the same problems as other advanced countries.

There are also other issues. On the up-side, U.S. farmers have been able to utilize advanced technology

クし、増やすことができるようになったということです。たとえばGPSを使えば、ピンポイントで天候をチェックでき、かんがいの必要性を知ることもできます。多くのアメリカおよび世界中で関心の的となっているのが、GMO（遺伝子組換え作物）の増加です。コーンや他の穀物類は大きな割合をGMOが占めています。GMOによる生産は、作物を病気から守り、収穫を増やすこともできます。ですが、長い先のことを考えると、環境だけでなく人間にどのような影響があるかも心配で、遺伝子組換え技術による作物を受け入れない人もいます。日本やヨーロッパでは、GMOによる食材の輸入に抵抗を示しています。ただし、アメリカの生産者はこの方針を変更するよう圧力をかけているのです。

Q　アメリカの今のIT産業はどうなっていますか？

90年代、シリコンバレーを筆頭に、IT産業は巨大産業に成長しました。そのことにより人々の生活は一変し、世界中のコミュニケーションも大きな変革を遂げました。

2011年の5月、IT業界の雄、マイクロソフト社がスカイプを買収しました。インターネットを介した電話やビデオ電話のソフトウェアを開発した会社です。こうした投資の流れは、想像できない

to monitor and increase their yields, with GPS-pin-pointed weather information to assist in irrigation decisions, for instance. One issue of concern to many in the U.S. and around the world is the increase in GMO products, now accounting for a vast majority of corn and other grain production. Genetic modification of crops to make them disease-resistant, or to increase yields, has led to concerns over the long-term impact both on the environment and on humans, with some insisting on Non-GMO products. Japan and European countries continue to resist imports of GMO foodstuffs, although they are under pressure from U.S. manufacturers to change their policies.

Q What is the current state of America's IT industry?

In the '90s, the IT business, and Silicon Valley in particular, grew into a huge industry that revolutionized people's lives and communications around the world.

In May 2011, the IT industry giant Microsoft bought Skype, a software application that allows users to make voice calls or have video chats over the Internet. This and other investments are having an incredible

ほどの影響をこの業界に与えました。20世紀の終わり頃、投資家たちはこぞってIT業界に投資しました。それが21世紀になって早々、いわゆる「ドット・コム・バブル」が弾け、アメリカの金融界は危機に直面したのです。しかし、今でも、ITが主要産業であることは変わらず、アメリカ人の毎日の生活や経済全体に大きな影響を与えているのです。

ITビジネスは、リスクをとるアメリカ人のパイオニア精神によく合っています。またこれにより世界中から移民が流れ込み、業界に優秀な人材が集まり、そこで働いているのです。IT業界のリーダーたちにとって、多くのインド人や他のアジアからの人たちがアメリカに移り住んでいることは、周知の事実なのです。

オンラインショップの雄アマゾン、検索エンジンの最高峰グーグル、そして超有名企業のマイクロソフトやアップルなど、すべてアメリカで起業された会社です。そして彼らのビジネスは世界中に広がっているのです。彼らこそがアメリカ経済の新しい礎なのです。

検索エンジン大手Yahoo本社

シリコンバレーの中心、サンノゼ市

effect in stimulating this futuristic industry. At the end of the twentieth century, however, speculators were putting too much money into the IT industry, and in the first months of the twenty-first century, the bursting of so-called "dot-com bubble" triggered a financial crisis in America. However, even today, IT is a major industry and has a huge influence on both the everyday lives of Americans and the overall economy.

The IT business is well suited to the pioneering, risk-taking American spirit, and it has also taken in immigrants from around the world, resulting in an industry that fosters the talents of the capable people who work in it. It is common knowledge that among the leaders in the IT industry, a great number come from India and other Asian countries.

Companies such as the on-line shopping giant Amazon, the industry-leading search engine Google, and the famous competitors Microsoft and Apple were all created in America, and these businesses have expanded all over the world. They are the new foundations of America's economy.

アメリカの経営と職場環境

Q アメリカでのセクハラとはどのような問題を指すのですか？

アメリカでは職場でのセクハラの問題がしばしば裁判所に持ち込まれています。アメリカでのセクハラは単に誰かが性的ないやがらせをしたといったような問題だけを指しているのではありません。例えば、誰かが職場のコンピュータに男性誌のヌードグラビアをダウンロードしていたとします。するとそれを目撃した女性が、女性を蔑視したその人の行為のために職場環境が不愉快なものになったとして会社に抗議します。この抗議を会社があいまいなまま放置しておくと、その女性が会社が無責任だと法的な措置に訴えることができるのです。

すなわち、アメリカでのセクハラのケースとは、職場において性的な理由で不愉快な思いをしたりすること全般に対して、職場での男女の平等を規定する法律に照らして審議される事柄なのです。

American Management and Office Environments

Q What does sexual harassment refer to in the USA?

It is quite common in America for sexual harassment to become the subject of court cases. It is not only a question of whether someone sexually harasses another person. For example, someone in the office may download a nude pin-up from a men's magazine into his computer. A woman who witnesses this can file a protest with the company, claiming that such behavior shows contempt for women and makes the office environment uncomfortable. If the company ignores her protest, she can take legal action, claiming an irresponsible attitude on the part of the company.

Sexual harassment in the US is thus an issue considered in reference to laws stipulating sexual equality at the workplace designed to counter situations that make the workplace uncomfortable for reasons related to sex.

Q 企業経営での「イコーリティ」の問題とはどのような ことなのですか？

　アメリカでの企業の運営において最も注意しなければならないことに、雇用機会均等法を遵守するということがあります。アメリカでは公民権法によって、職場における人種、性別、信教、身体の障害の有無、出身国などを理由として人を差別したり不愉快な思いを与えたりしてはいけないということが定められているからです。また州によっては同性愛などといった個人の性的な嗜好、あるいは年齢などによる差別を禁止しているところもありあます。

　人を平等に扱うという大前提に従ってできあがったこの法律の拘束力は大変強く、経営者は、職場での全ての差別を排除して、快適な職場環境を創造するよう義務づけられているのです。そして、従業員も、平等、すなわち「イコーリティ」の原則に従って、何か問題があれば、例え相手が上司であろうが、はたまた経営者であろうが、この法律での規定と精神に則って、抗議することに躊躇しません。これが、企業経営での「イコーリティ」に対して経営者が神経を使う背景なのです。

Q アメリカでの労働時間はどのようになっていますか？

　アメリカ人は５時になればさっさと職場を離れるというのは、多少ステレオタイプなイメージと

Q What is equal opportunity in corporate management?

One of the issues American corporate management has to pay a great deal of attention to is observation of the equal opportunity law. This civil rights law stipulates that no one should suffer discrimination nor discomfort in the workplace on grounds of race, gender, religion, physical disability, or country of origin. Some states also prohibit discrimination against homosexuality and other private sexual matters, as well as age.

The law was established with its main premise as equal treatment for all. It has strong binding powers that essentially oblige management to abolish all discrimination in the workplace to create a pleasant working environment. Employees do not hesitate to raise complaints about their boss, or even company owners, if any problem arises under the law or the spirit of the law. Corporate equality is thus something about which management exercises a lot of thought.

Q What are American working hours?

It is a bit of a cliche to imagine that Americans leave the office as soon as 5:00 p.m. comes around. Some

いえそうです。アメリカでも人によっては長時間働きますし、必要ならば休日出勤なども平気です。特に都市部の中小のベンチャー企業に働く人の労働時間は相当長くなっているようです。ただ、大きな会社にはユニオンなどの規定もあり、労働時間が厳密に規定されている組織もあるようです。

　一般的には、アメリカでの労働時間は、与えられた業務をちゃんと遂行している以上、個人の責任にかかっているというのが常識で、もちろん、他の社員との人間関係の育成やグループ活動のために残業をするといった日本のような風習はまったくありません。仕事が終われば、あとは個人の時間というのがアメリカの常識なのです。

　これはしばしば「仕事と生活のバランス」を正しく維持することにつながります。ひとつの方法として、アメリカではフレックス制や在宅勤務が推奨されます。家族との時間を最大化するために、出社時間や帰宅時間を自分で決めるのです。もしくは家から仕事をすることで、時間、コスト、そして環境的にも影響を軽減する働き方があります。

Q　アメリカでの賃金水準はどのようになっているのですか？

　2015年の統計によれば、アメリカ全体の1人当たりの年間所得平均は5万6,083ドルです。しかし、アメリカでは給与水準の格差は大変大きく、経営

people work long hours and think nothing of coming to the office on weekends if necessary. The workdays of people in venture businesses in urban areas are very long indeed. Large corporations, however, have strictly fixed working hours in accordance with union regulations.

Generally, working hours are considered a matter of individual responsibility, just as long as the allocated task gets done. No custom exists in the US for staying after-hours in order to develop relationships with colleagues or participate in group activities, as in Japan. In the USA people believe that the hours after work should be spent on one's personal life.

This is often referred to as maintaining a proper "work-life balance." One way this is accomplished in the U.S. is through flex-time or telecommuting—by which workers can adjust the hours they arrive at and leave the office in order to maximize time with their families, or even work from their "home office," thereby avoiding the time, expense, and environmental impact of commuting.

Q What is the wage standard in the US?

According to 2015 statistics, the annual average income per person in the US is $56,083. The wage differential, however, is very great, and it is not unusual for the

者と一般の従業員との収入の差が100万ドル以上というケースも珍しくはありません。アメリカの平等の原則は誰でも才能があればそうした栄華を勝ち取れるという機会にたいする平等が保障されているというものですから、この給与水準の格差が是正されることはあまり期待できません。

　また、地方によって給与水準に大きな格差があるのも事実で、最も平均所得の低いミシシッピ州と、高いとされるニューハンプシャー州との格差は約3万ドルにもなるのです。現在アメリカでは貧富の差が拡大していることが1つの社会問題となっています。2016年、この議論により、ワシントン州を筆頭にしたいくつかの州で、労働者の最低賃金を引き上げることで少しでも格差を是正し、生活上の困難を軽減しようとしたのです。また、法の上で男女の平等が確立したからといえ、実際には大学院を卒業した女性の平均収入は同じクラスの男性の約70％に過ぎないといった事実もあります。こうした賃金格差の問題は、平等の問題を考えて行く上で、今後の大きな課題の1つとなりそうです。

Q　アメリカ式経営の特徴として挙げられるものにどのようなものがありますか？

　アメリカでの経営の特徴は、何といっても従業員の能力と契約するという形で人を雇い、いった

difference between management and the more general worker to be as much as $1 million. Since it is a principle of American equality that anybody with talent can succeed and become rich, it is highly unlikely that the wage differential will disappear.

There is also a big difference in wage standard according to region. The differential between Mississippi, the state with the lowest average income, and New Hampshire, with the highest, amounts to $30,000. Wealth disparity is increasing in the US, and it has become a social problem. In 2016, this debate has led some states—led by Washington State—to increase the minimum wage workers should receive, in order to reduce the gap and permit families to get by with less difficulty. Gender equality has been established by law, but the average income of a woman with a master's degree is roughly 70% of that of a man with the same education. The wage differential is currently an important equality issue.

Q What are some characteristics of the way Americans run businesses?

The most notable characteristic of American business practice is probably the way people are employed on the

んその人を雇ったら、その人の実績のみをチェックし、あとは極力その人の自由と独立性を尊重するというマネージメント方法にあるのではないでしょうか。

　もちろん、実績をチェックするときに、改善点などについて適切なアドバイスを与えるのは上司の重要な役割ですが、その後の方法論については本人の選択と自主性に任されます。

　日本では新卒を採用し、長い年月をかけてその人をプロとして育てていく方式をとりますが、アメリカでは従業員を育てるという方式はとりません。会社としては教育等の機会は提供しますが、能力を伸ばしキャリアをアップさせるのはあくまでも個人の責任で、必要であれば本人が会社に対して教育の機会を与えてもらうよう提案していきます。

　従って、逆に従業員が契約通りの業績をあげられない場合、あるいは従業員が自らの仕事や待遇に満足できない場合は、双方が契約の在り方について交渉し、時によっては雇用関係を打ち切ることも充分にありうるのです。

basis of capability. Once they are employed, evaluation is made solely on their achievement. Also, high priority is given to employees' freedom and independence.

Of course, superiors must point out areas where improvement can be made when the time for evaluation comes around, but the method is left up to the employee's discretion.

Japanese companies use a method of employing recent graduates and educating them over time in the job. In the US, companies do not nurture employees in the same way. Companies provide the opportunity for growth, but fostering one's abilities and career is always left up to individual responsibility. If necessary, employees can ask for certain education opportunities to be provided by the company.

So when employees do not live up to their contract, or if they are dissatisfied with their jobs or treatment, both sides can renegotiate the contract, and sometimes the contract is simply broken by one side.

◆コラム◆ アメリカの世界企業の強さとは

　アップルなどに代表されるアメリカ企業の強さは、なんといっても世界中の知恵をそこに集めていることにあります。

　シリコンバレーなどに行けば、先端企業で働いている人々がいかに多様かということに驚かされます。

　最近では、ヨーロッパ各地に加え、アジアや中近東からの人々が、そうした企業の戦力として活動しているのです。企業の敷地の中を歩けば、ここがアメリカなのかと思えるほどに、様々な顔や言語に接することができます。企業周辺には、世界中のレストランなどが集まり、そうした人々の生活と交流を支えています。

　現在では企業の中に海外からの移住者がしっかりとした層となり、中堅幹部に、さらにはトップの管理職までが、移民の厚い層の中から輩出されるようになりました。世界の知恵が集まり、世界の風俗習慣への情報が集積することによって、アメリカの企業は日々新陳代謝を繰り返しているのです。

　アメリカ企業にはアメリカ国籍でなければという血統主義は存在しません。優秀であれば、昇進の機会は民族や国籍に関係なく与えられます。さらに、そうした人材のプールとなる研究機関や大学なども、積極的に世界中から人々をリクルートしているのです。

　また、本部の下に支社があるといったピラミッド型の組織構造ではなく、世界中にネットワークしながら現地支社の現場から、関係する部門が直接レポートを受けられる柔軟な構造が育っていることも、アメリカ企業の特徴です。

　人種や性別への差別のないフラットな企業構造。そんな環境に憧れて、さらに海外から多くの人材が集まるのが、アメリカの先端をいく企業の特徴なのです。

Chapter 5

Society—Life

第5章　社会・生活

アメリカの生活環境

Q アッパーミドル・クラスとロー・インカム・ファミリーとの関係は？

アメリカは平等を原則とする国家ですから、社会制度としての階級は存在しません。しかし、最近では国民の間の貧富の差や教育程度の差などが顕著になり、階級ではなく階層の分化が顕著になってきているといわれています。

アメリカでの階層の対立を象徴する問題としてよく取り上げられるのが、アッパーミドル・クラスとロー・インカム・ファミリーとの関係です。

アメリカ人はよく社会が2極に分化されているといいます。いわゆる中産階級、特に都市部などで裕福に暮らすアッパーミドル・クラスと、同じ都市部にあって、スラム化した地域に生活するロー・インカム・ファミリー、すなわち低所得者層との確執は、アメリカの大きな社会問題になっています。貧しいところに生まれれば、その地域自体に資金がないために、学校の設備も立ち遅れ、子供の教育にも支障をきたします。教育にかかる費用はほとんど地方自治体の税金でまかなわれるからです。教育を十分に受けられない子供たちは街にたむろして犯罪や麻薬へと走り、そのことが

The American Living Environment

Q What is the relationship between upper-middle class and low-income families?

America is a country based on the principle of equality, so no social system of class exists. Recently, however, a significant disparity has arisen in wealth and educational background, and divisions between social strata are definitely noticeable.

The relationship between the upper-middle class and low-income families is often cited as an example of the difference between social strata.

Americans often say that their society is polarized into two groups. There are the upper-middle classes, which are those who live affluently, particularly in urban areas, and the low-income families, who live in slum sections of the same urban areas. This distinct division is becoming a major social problem. Children born into the poor segments of the population suffer disadvantages in terms of education, as most educational expenses are raised through local taxes. Insufficient school facilities exist due to these communities' lack of financial resources. Children without a chance of an adequate education hang around in the

さらに他のコミュニティと彼等とを隔絶させていくことになります。

このように、アメリカでは、持てるものと持たざるものとの対立が、日々深刻になってきています。悪循環をどのようにして断ち切るか、教育問題をどのようにして解決して、都市のスラム化を防止するか。これは今後アメリカが取り組まなければならない最も重要な課題の1つなのです。

Q アメリカでは同性愛者は平等に扱われているのですか？

アメリカで同性愛者の権利が強調されはじめたのは1960年代の後半のことです。人をその人の性の嗜好で差別してはいけないという考え方を、いわゆる公民権運動の1つとして展開し、同性愛者だということで就職できなかったり解雇されたり、あるいは嫌がらせをうけることは人権の侵害だということが運動を通して訴えられたのです。1975年に、政府機関で同性愛者に差別なく就職や昇進の機会を与えることが保障され、その後の数十年で差別は減少してきました。とはいえ、完全になくなったわけではないのです。

最近では同性愛者も法律の上ではかなり平等に扱われるようになり、職業上での差別等は違法行為として雇用者が罰せ

ニューヨークで行われたゲイ・パレード

streets, get caught up in crimes and drugs, and these communities become even more alienated from others than before.

The conflict between the "haves" and the "have-nots" grows more serious day by day. The most important issue to be dealt with in the US is how to stop this vicious cycle—how to solve the problem of areas with underfunded education and how to prevent the cities' slide into urban decay.

Q Do gay people receive equal treatment in the US?

It was in the late 1960s that gay rights came to the forefront. The idea that no one should be discriminated against because of their sexuality developed into a kind of civil rights movement. Gay rights campaigners lobbied that job rejection, dismissal, or harassment based on homosexuality was a violation of human rights. Equal opportunities without discrimination for jobs and promotion in government was guaranteed in 1975. Discrimination against gays has been decreasing in recent decades, but has not disappeared altogether.

In recent years, homosexual people have come into considerable protection under the law. Discrimination at job sites is illegal, and employers will be punished if

られるようになりました。特に近年では軍隊に同性愛者を受け入れるべきかという論争も展開され、採用の際に同性愛者であるかどうかを問いかけないという方針が打ち出されました。

さらに、現在話題となっているのは、同性愛者同士の結婚を法的に認めるかどうかというテーマです。現在のところ法律上結婚を承認している州はありません。ただ、今後この問題はさらにクローズアップされてくるのではと思われます。

Q アメリカではどのような都市や地域に人気があるのですか？

現代的なビルと自然が混合したシアトルの街

自然豊かなアスペンの中心地

アメリカ人に人気のある場所は、温暖で海や山がそばにあるシアトル、ロッキー山脈の懐に抱かれたアスペンなどのコロラドの街々、老後の生活の定番となっているフロリダ州ウエストパームビーチなどの諸都市、さらには風光明媚で温暖なサンフランシスコ、カナダに近く、東海岸の都市の喧騒を嫌った人たちの移動先として知られる、ニューイングランド地方のバーモント州などが挙げられます。

最近、様々な都市問題を抱えるロサンゼルスに代表されるカリフォルニアの都

it is seen to exist. The issue of whether gays should be accepted in the military has been the subject of much debate. In the 1990s, a "Don't Ask, Don't Tell" policy was adopted, in which recruiters do not inquire about sexuality in recruitment interviews. However, this policy is now pending repeal in the federal government.

Another recent issue has been whether to legally recognize gay marriages. Currently, gay marriage is not recognized legally in most American states, but the issue is likely to undergo greater attention in the future.

Q Which cities and areas in the US are the most popular?

The most popular places to live for Americans are Seattle, with its mild climate close to the mountains and ocean, Aspen and other Colorado towns in the bosom of the Rockies, West Palm Beach and other cities in Florida, which are great retirement places, San Francisco, with its mild climate and beautiful scenery, and the New England state of Vermont, which is close to Canada and a perfect place to get away from the bustle of East Coast cities.

Recent reports say that people living in big cities like Los Angeles and New York are moving out to

市部、あるいはニューヨークなどから人が流出している
という報道が何度かありました。特に、コンピュータ・ネットワークを利用して、田舎で生活しながら、必要な時には近くの空港から出張するというライフスタイルもはやっていて、そうした人たちが、脱都会組の先駆けとなっているようです。思いもつかないところでは、ラスベガスの人口急増があります。

宗 教

Q アメリカでの宗教の特徴とはどのようなものですか？

　アメリカには、ヨーロッパでの迫害に追われ、自由な新天地を求めて海を渡ってきたプロテスタントの人々がまず根付きました。その後も、ヨーロッパ各地からプロテスタントの人々が移住し、現在でもアメリカでのプロテスタント系のキリスト教の影響は大変大きなものといえそうです。

　ミズーリやカンザスなどといった中西部は、特にプロテスタント教会の力が根強い地域で、この地域は、別名バイブル・ベルト地帯と呼ばれています。

　一方、19世紀になってからは、アイルランドやイタリアといったカトリック系の移民も多くやっ

the countryside to live. Here, they can telecommute via Internet, and when occasion demands they go into their workplace from the local airports. These people seem to be the precursors of an exodus from the cities. One unlikely destination that has seen considerable population growth is Las Vegas.

Religion

Q What are the characteristics of religion in the USA?

It was the Protestants who first came across the ocean from Europe in search of a free, new world and settled in America. Later, many more Protestants emigrated from various parts of Europe, and their influence is still strong in the US today.

In certain regions of the Mid-West, such as Missouri or Kansas, the Protestant Church still has a great influence. This area is often called the "Bible Belt."

In the nineteenth century, a great number of Catholic immigrants came from Ireland, Italy, and

てきました。現在では6,950万人にものぼるカトリック系の人々がアメリカで生活しています。

最近では、アメリカでも宗教に対して疑問を抱き、教会に通わなくなった世代が増えてきたといわれています。また、1960年代以降、都市部を中心に仏教やイスラム教といったアメリカ人にとっては新しい宗教が浸透し、特に黒人の間では、自らのルーツを主張するためにイスラム教に帰依した人もかなりいます。

とはいっても、大統領の就任式で大統領が聖書に手を置いて宣誓する習わしからも、やはりキリスト教がアメリカを代表する宗教であることには変わりはないようです。

1985年、聖書に手をおき宣誓するレーガン大統領

Q プロテスタントとはどのような宗教なのですか？

プロテスタントは16世紀にマルティン・ルターがドイツでカトリックを批判し、それに対抗して起こした宗教です。強大な力をもっていたローマ教皇から異端とされ、迫害を受けますが、逆にローマの影響力からの離脱を狙うヨーロッパの王侯の多くに支持を受け、このことにより、ヨーロッパを二分する動乱が長々と続くことになります。また、マルティン・ルターのあと、様々なプロテスタント系宗派が現れ、ヨーロッパ各地に点在したことも、事態をさらに複雑なものにしていきました。

other countries. There are now as many as 69.5 million Catholics in the US.

Recently the younger generations hold religion in a kind of suspicion, and fewer people are attending church. There has been an increase in religions new to North America, such as Buddhism, Islam, etc., especially in urban areas. Many black people in particular have become Muslims, identifying with their places of origin.

But as we see from such ceremonies as the Presidential Inauguration, where the president puts his hand on the Bible to take the oath, the influence of Christianity in the US is still strong.

Q What kind of religion is Protestantism?

Protestantism is the religion Martin Luther started in Germany in the sixteenth century, protesting in opposition to Catholicism. It was designated as heresy by the Vatican, which had tremendous power, and its followers were persecuted. But many kings in Europe who wanted to escape the Vatican's influence gave it support. A long period of upheaval in Europe followed when the continent was divided between the two major strands of Christianity. Various sects of Protestantism scattered all over Europe and further complicated the situation.

その結果、迫害を受けたり、追放されたりした
プロテスタントが新大陸を目指して旅立ったので
す。彼等にとって、汚されていないアメリカ大陸
は、まさに神が与えてくれた「プロミスト・ランド」
でした。

また、プロテスタントの多くは労働を信仰の一
部としていることもあって、彼等は新大陸で勤勉
に働き、さかんに開墾事業を進め、様々なビジネ
スを起こしました。プロテスタントの信仰とそこ
で育まれた価値観こそが、アメリカの発展の原動
力の1つとなっていったのです。

Q モルモン教とはどのような教会ですか？

モルモン教は1830年にジョセフ・スミスによっ
て、ニューヨーク州の北部で創立されたアメリカ
生まれの宗教です。モルモン教の正式名称は、末
日聖徒イエス・キリスト教会となります。

アメリカはその昔神が訪れ、キリストをはじめ
多くの聖人が訪れた大地であるという独特の教義
のもと、アメリカに神が残したとされるブック・
オブ・モルモン（モルモン書）を聖典として重視し、
神の国が新大陸に樹立されると説くのがモルモン
教の特徴です。

彼等は、そのユニークな信仰のため、また一夫
多妻制をとる宗教であったことなどが影響して、
あちこちで迫害を受け、ニューヨーク州を捨てて

It was these Protestants who had suffered persecution and exile that set sail for the New World. For them, the great continent was virgin territory—here, they thought, was the "promised land," given to them by God.

Protestant people have a strong work ethic—labor is part of their creed. They worked diligently in the new land, carrying out development projects and starting various businesses. Protestant beliefs and the values nurtured by them were an important fuel that helped America come about.

Q What is the Mormon Church?

The Mormon religion was founded by Joseph Smith in 1830 in the northern part of New York. It is thus a religion born in America. Its official name is the Church of Jesus Christ of Latter-day Saints.

Mormon doctrine holds that God, Jesus Christ, and many of the saints walked on American soil in ancient times. The Book of Mormon, given by God, is its sacred book. The Mormon religion preaches that the land of God will be established in the New World.

Mormons were persecuted in many places because of the religion's unique doctrine and its acceptance of polygamy. Many Mormons moved to Ohio, or Illinois,

オハイオ州やイリノイ州へと転々とし、最終的には1847年に現在のユタ州のソルトレイクシティに安住の地を見出し、定住しました。

その後連邦政府のすすめもあって、一夫多妻制は19世紀の末に廃止されました。モルモン教は伝道活動にも熱心で、日本にも積極的に宣教師を派遣しています。現在、モルモン教の信者はアメリカだけで460万人。現在でもユタ州の人口の70％はモルモン教の人々であるといわれています。

ソルトレイクシティにあるモルモン教の総本山

Q アメリカのカトリックにはどのような地盤があるのですか？

アメリカでカトリックの人々が増加しはじめたのは、19世紀の半ば以降、アイルランドやイタリアからの移民が大量に海を渡って来るようになってからです。それ以前は圧倒的にプロテスタントで占められていました。

また、最近ではメキシコ、カリブ、その他の中南米の国々からスペインの影響を受けた大量のカトリック系移民がアメリカで生活しています。現在、カトリック系の総人口は約6,800万人。カトリック系の大統領としてはケネディが知られていますが、レーガン大統領も母親はプロテスタントでしたが、カトリックだった父親の影響も受けていると言われています。

and eventually, in 1847, found a place to settle in Salt Lake City, Utah.

The system of polygamy was abandoned at the end of the nineteenth century, with encouragement from the federal government. Mormons are enthusiastic evangelists. They have dispatched many missionaries to Japan. Mormon believers total 4.6 million in the US, and 70% of the Utah population is said to be Mormon.

Q What kind of base does Catholicism have in the USA?

Catholicism began to increase around the mid-nineteenth century, with the great influx of immigrants from Ireland and Italy. Before that time, most immigrants were Protestants.

Recent Catholic immigrants have come from Mexico, the Caribbean, and other Latin American countries, areas that previously were under the influence of Spain. Catholics total 68 million. President Kennedy was a Catholic believer, and President Reagan's father was Catholic, leaving an imprint, mixed with his mother's Protestantism.

Q アメリカには宗教の違いによる対立はあるのですか？

アメリカには昔はヨーロッパほど苛烈ではないにしろ、宗教弾圧もあれば、迫害もありました。しかし、アメリカの憲法が制定され、信教の自由が謳われて以来、そうしたケースは殆どなくなりました。ただ、宗教が唱える信条の違いによる対立は今でも深刻な問題を引き起こしています。代表的な例は、人工妊娠中絶は殺人行為だとする人々と、個人の判断によって決めることで、宗教や政治が介入する問題ではないとする人々との対立です。

中絶反対を唱える人々は、キリスト教を強く信仰し、その哲学を政治にも教育にも反映させるべきだという立場の人が多く、彼等の中には、中絶を行うクリニックに対してテロ行為に出たりする人もいるほどです。

もともと、宗教の違いは、そのまま人種の違いに繋がっているケースも多く、宗教対立が人種偏見を苛烈なものにしたこともありました。ただ、こうした宗教や人種を露骨に差別する行為は1964年に公民権法が制定されて以来、極めて少なくなってきたようです。

中東へのアメリカの関与、そしてイスラム原理主義の台頭により、最近の傾向としてアメリカ国

Q Are there religious conflicts in the USA?

Although religious conflict was not as intense as in Europe, historically, religious suppression has occurred in the US, as has friction between religions. But after the promulgation of the Constitution, which extolled freedom of religion, such occurrences became less frequent. Doctrinal differences, and differences concerning ethics, however, do give rise to serious confrontations. The most significant example surrounds the issue of abortion. The anti-abortionists claim that abortion is murder, while the pro-abortionists think that the matter should be left up to the individual, without religious or political intervention.

Those opposing abortion are mostly firm believers in Christianity, who advocate that the Christian faith should be reflected in politics and education. Some of them are so adamant that they carry out terrorist acts against abortion clinics.

Religious differences are often directly tied with differences between races. Religious confrontation has often inflamed racial prejudice. But cases of blatant discrimination based on religion or race have become much fewer since the establishment of civil rights in 1964.

Given the nature of American involvement in the Middle East, and the rise of Islamic fundamentalism,

内のイスラム教徒への注目が集まっています。イスラム教徒への差別が増加したのです。とはいえ、社会の指導的立場にいる人たちはイスラム教徒を保護し、アメリカの宗教の自由という原則を強調しようとしているのです。

アメリカの社会問題

Q アメリカでのドラッグの問題はどれくらい深刻なのですか？

　2008年の統計によると、ドラッグ関係の事件で逮捕された人の数は全米で130万4,100人となっています。ただし、ドラッグが原因で別の凶悪犯罪に走った人の数を入れれば、その数は何倍にも膨れ上がります。

　大都市にはシューティング・ギャラリーと呼ばれる、麻薬を回し打つ密会所があります。こうしたところには中南米などから密輸されるクラックと呼ばれる中毒性の高い麻薬が出回っています。1回の注射の料金は20ドル程といわれていますが、中毒すると常用するようになるので、瞬く間に資産を使い果たし、家庭が崩壊してしまいます。さらに、注射針を回し打つことからエイズへの感染率も高く、このことがもう1つの社会問題となっ

one trend in recent years has been an increased focus on Muslims in the U.S. Instances of discrimination against Muslims have been on the rise, but civic leaders have sought to protect them and emphasize America's principles of religious freedom.

American Social Problems

Q How serious is the drug problem in the USA?

According to 2008 statistics, the total number of drug-related arrests reached 1,304,100. If one adds the number of people involved in serious drug-related crimes, the figure soars.

In the bigger cities there are places called "shooting galleries," where people meet secretly and shoot each other up with drugs. Strong drugs like "crack" smuggled from Latin America are freely available there. A single hit costs about $20, but once a person is addicted, he or she can lose everything in the need to buy more, and whole families are destroyed. Also, people share injection needles, which heightens the risk of AIDS infection, another social problem.

ています。

　貧困層にとっては、ドラッグは単に日々の苦し
みから逃れるだけのものではありません。ギャン
グの片棒をかついで、それを密売すれば、たちま
ちまとまったキャッシュが手に入るのです。こう
したことから、ドラッグ・ビジネスに走り、ギャ
ングの抗争に巻き込まれ、命を落としたり、刑務
所に入ったりする人も増えています。

　ドラッグは、アメリカ社会を蝕む、最も深刻な
問題の1つなのです。

Q　アメリカでは人種の対立はどのような社会問題を引き起こしているのですか？

　アメリカでの人種の対立は、時には暴動といっ
たような悲しい事件の原因になっています。特に、
白人系の人々と黒人やマイノリティの人々との対
立が原因で、数多く暴力事件が発生しています。
1992年の、黒人の青年が白人の警察官に暴行され、
その警察官が裁判で無罪になったことに怒った暴
徒がロサンゼルスを焼き打ちにしたロサンゼルス
暴動などはそうした例の1つです。

　さらに最近では、警察が黒人を殺害する事件が
顕著になっています。そばにいた人がスマートフォ
ンで録画した動画が流れたのです。社会は警察官
に対する敬意と、警察の権利——時には命まで奪
う——で引き裂かれています。そしておうおうに

For the poorer segments of society, drugs are not only a method of escaping from the pain of daily existence, but also, if one belongs to a gang, a way to earn considerable amounts of cash. The number of people who enter the drug business and get involved in gang disputes, eventually getting killed or being sent to prison, is increasing.

Drugs is one the most serious problems gnawing away at American society.

Q What kinds of social problems does racial confrontation cause in the US?

Racial confrontation can be the cause of tragic incidents and disturbances. Confrontations between Whites and Blacks or other minority groups have been behind many violent incidents. One example occurred in May of 1992, when riots erupted in Los Angeles minutes after an all-White jury acquitted LA police officers on charges of beating a Black man. Sections of the city were burnt to ashes by angry rioters.

In more recent years, the flash-point has been the killing of Black individuals by police, caught on video by bystanders using their Smart Phones. Society has been torn by its respect for the "Men & Women in Blue" (the police), yet their denial of rights—and

してそれは人種差別が起こしていることなのです。

　しかし、何よりも深刻なのは、暴動などに発展しないまでも、アメリカの社会に歴然と残る人種間の不信感ではないでしょうか。これは統計など表面には現れない心理的な事柄だけに、なかなか一朝一夕には解決できません。そしてこの不信感がもとで、思わぬことが差別事件などに発展するケースもあるのです。

　人種の違いを元に人を傷つけたり差別したりすることは法律で厳しく禁止されています。しかし、こうした犯罪が後を絶たないのもアメリカの人種問題の根深さを物語っています。ちなみに、2009年のFBIによる調査では、人種や宗教そして性別（同性愛者への犯罪も含む）に起因した犯罪が6,604件報告されています。

Q　アメリカでの銃の規制はどのようになっているのですか？

　アメリカで2008年に殺人事件の犠牲になった人の数は1万4,299人です。そして、そのうちの7割は銃によって命を奪われました。アメリカは、その昔イギリスの抑圧に民衆が武器を持って立ち上がり、独立を勝ちえた経緯があります。さらに荒野を開拓するなかで、銃が身を守り、狩りをするための必需品であったことから、武器を所有する権利を主張する根強い世論があります。銃を保有

sometimes of life itself—that often seems racially motivated.

But the most serious element is probably the distrust that still exists among races in US society—even when it doesn't develop into riots. There are psychological aspects to the problem which resist statistic analysis, making easy solutions impossible. And since suspicion and distrust do exist, incidents can develop out of the slightest matters.

Injuring others or discriminating against them on racial grounds is strictly prohibited by law. Yet crimes related to racial discrimination never cease, which shows just how deep-rooted racial problems are in the US. For example, 6,604 crimes related to racial, religious, and gender discrimination were reported by the FBI in 2009.

Q What is the status of gun control in the US?

There were 14,299 murder victims in the US in 2008. Roughly 70% of these were killed by a gun. The opinion that people have the right to possess guns in the US remains strong. The reasons behind it stem from the fact that Americans won independence from Britain with arms, and in the pioneer period guns were necessary for self-protection and hunting. The right to own guns is enshrined in the Second Amendment

する権利は、合衆国憲法の修正第2条にうたわれています。そのため、銃の保有を制限することは、憲法の条文である銃保持の権利に抗うことになるのです。

とはいえ、凶悪犯罪の増加によって、連邦政府は銃を購入するときに、売り手が再考を促すことを義務づけるなどの法案を可決しました。また、例えばニューヨークのように、地域によっては銃をコントロールするための強い法律を施行しているところもあります。しかし、テキサス州などはそうした動きに真っ向から対立し、なかなか銃規制は思うように進んではいません。

銃の規制の是非は、アメリカ人の個人の権利と公共の福祉という2つのテーマの中で世論を二分している問題なのです。

Q　アメリカでの 犯罪の実状はどのようになっていますか？

アメリカでの凶悪犯罪がいかに深刻な問題であるかはすでに、日本でも何度も報道されています。特に銃を使用した犯罪、麻薬関係、そして人種や性、そして子供など弱者に対する犯罪はアメリカが最も悩み、解決を模索している犯罪です。2008年の統計によると、同年に何らかの犯罪に関わって逮捕された人の延べ人数は1,100万人です。

教育問題や人種問題に加え、最近では失業やストレスなどからくる精神障害が元での犯罪も目

to the nation's Constitution, so any effort to restrain gun-ownership is challenged as being opposed to the Constitutionally guaranteed right to own weapons.

For all that, an increase of atrocious crimes has led Congress to pass a bill stipulating that gun-sellers must urge buyers to reconsider at the time of purchase. Some areas like New York do enforce strict gun control laws. Others like Texas completely oppose gun control, which shows no chance of advance there.

Gun control is a difficult issue in the US. Public opinion is split between individual rights and the public welfare.

Q What is the current state of crime in the US?

The serious crime problem in the US has been reported many times in Japan. Particularly troubling are the crimes involving guns and drugs, race-related and sex-related crimes, and crimes against defenseless members of society, like children. According to 2008 statistics, arrests for crimes totaled 11.1 million.

In addition to educational or racial problems, mental disorders caused by job loss or stress are becoming

立ってきています。社会が複雑になり、人と人との疎外が進む中で、悲劇が起きているのです。特に、都市部での犯罪は相変わらず深刻です。特に犯罪率の高い地域とされるワシントンD.C.での10万人あたりの殺人件数は78件、強姦が56件、強盗が1,230件となっています。

ただ、忘れほしくないのは、大部分のアメリカは安全で人々が健全に暮らしているということです。こうした安全なアメリカをいかに守っていくかというテーマをめぐって、より強い法律と警察力を導入するべきだという人と、もっと福祉や教育に力をいれるべきだという人との間で、激しい政策論争が展開されているのも事実なのです。

Q アメリカでの失業率はどのように推移しているのですか？

リーマン・ショックによって引きおこされた景気後退後、最も失業率が高かったのは、2010年の9.6％でした。この数字はアメリカ史上最悪の失業率を記録した1982年の10.8％に匹敵します。最近の失業率は、2008年の経済危機が要因で、アメリカはまだこの時の後遺症に悩んでいるのです。

とはいえ、失業率を詳しく分析してみると、2008年の白人の失業率が4.4％であったのに対し

another cause of crime. The world is becoming more complex and people feel increasingly alienated, which sometimes leads to tragic incidents. Urban crimes are more serious than ever. Washington, D.C. is a place with a particularly high crime rate: 78 murder cases in a population of 100,000, 56 rapes, and 1,230 cases of burglary.

But we should bear in mind that most of the US is safe with people living there quite peacefully. There is now an intensive political debate among people who advocate the incorporation of stronger law and police power to ensure public order, and people who argue that the funding for such a project would be better spent on welfare and education.

Q How is the US unemployment rate changing?

The unemployment rate following the Lehman Shock-induced recession was sky-high at 9.6% in 2010. This rivals the unemployment rate of 1982, which at 10.8% holds the record for highest unemployment rate in US history. The current unemployment is due to the economic crash of 2008, from which the US is still recovering.

A closer look at the figures, however, shows the unemployment rate of whites in 2008 as 4.4% while

て、黒人の失業率は9.2%、ヒスパニック系の人々は6.3%にもなり、人種間による格差が長きにわたって続く問題となっています。

家庭とコミュニティ

Q アメリカでは地域コミュニティはどのような活動をしていますか？

　アメリカでは伝統的にコミュニティ活動が大変さかんです。特に子供の教育を通して親同士が共同して活動し、土曜日などはバスケットボールや野球のリトルリーグなどを親が持ち回りで協力しあいながら運営したり、様々なボランティア活動に参加したりしています。こうしたコミュニティ活動の中心となるのが、学校や教会などで、必要ならば、子供の教育やその時の地域の課題などについてもその場で意見を交換したりします。

　この地域のコミュニティ活動は、その昔入植者たちが自らの地域のことを自分たちで話し合って決定していた伝統にもつながる、アメリカ人にとっての民主主義の核ともなる貴重な活動なのです。

that of blacks was 9.2% and 6.3% for Hispanics. The racial unemployment gap continues to be a long-standing issue.

Family and Community

Q What kind of community activities are there in the US?

There is a thriving tradition of community activities in the US. Parents participate in activities related to their children's education, taking turns managing the children's basketball team or the Little League on the weekends. They also participate in many other volunteer activities. The centers of these community activities are usually schools or churches, which also, if occasion demands, provide the place for exchanges of views on local issues, such as children's education.

Community activity plays an important role as the core of democracy in US society. It has its origins in the meetings colonists held to discuss and make decisions about issues affecting the community.

Q アメリカのボランティア活動はどのようになっていますか?

アメリカでは非常に積極的にボランティア活動が行われています。子供はボランティア活動に参加することを教育の一環として奨励されますし、お年寄りも自分の余暇を社会のためにと積極的に活動に加わります。

例えば、地域の病院での患者の世話や清掃、学校での子供への教育活動への参加、あるいはホームレスの人々への給食活動や、社会福祉施設への協力など、自分のできることなら何でも参加し、世の中に貢献しようというコミュニティ意識がこうしたボランティア活動を支えているのです。

企業もまた社会貢献を熱心に行います。企業単位でも適宜募金活動を行ったり、企業の収益の一部を社会福祉事業や博物館などの運営資金にあてたりといったことも頻繁に行われています。こうした活動は「企業の社会的責任」としてボランティア活動の精神にも通じるところがあるようです。

Q 「ファミリー・バリュー」とはどのような価値のことですか?

アメリカでは一時「ファミリー・バリュー」、すなわち家族の価値という考え方がさかんに議論され、1992年の大統領選挙では共和党側のスローガンの1つにもなりました。家庭の崩壊こそが教育

Q What is the status of volunteer activity in the US?

Americans are very active in volunteer work. Children are encouraged to take part in volunteer activities as a part of their education. Senior citizens also take an active role, using their leisure time for the betterment of society.

A community consciousness and the desire to contribute underlies this volunteer work. Activities include taking care of patients and cleaning at local hospitals, participating in children's education at schools, distributing food to the homeless, and helping at welfare facilities.

Companies are also enthusiastic in making their own kind of contribution. They raise funds, and frequently donate part of their revenues for welfare or museum management. Those corporate activities—known as Corporate Social Responsibility (CSR)—seem to have something in common with the spirit of volunteering.

Q What are "family values"?

"Family values" have been the subject of much public debate, and in 1992 they even became a Republican slogan in the presidential election. The restoration of such "family values" was seen as the solution for current

を疲弊させ、子供の犯罪や地域社会の腐敗につながるという意見が「ファミリー・バリュー」の議論の背景にありました。すなわち、現代社会の問題点にメスを入れるためには、勤勉で信仰にあつい父親と母親がいて、両親を尊敬し、学校で学び、地域の活動にも積極的な子供がいるようなアメリカの伝統的な家庭の在り方を取り戻そうというのが、この「ファミリー・バリュー」のテーマだったのです。

　一方で、このテーマは現代の世の中の実情に合わず、古典的な価値観だけを強調し、女性が母親としてではなく、社会人として活動していく男女同権の考え方などに逆行するものだという批判の対象ともなりました。

　また、単に「ファミリー・バリュー」だけを強調することは、いたずらに社会の保守化を招き、臭いものに蓋をしようとするだけだという批判もありました。

　ただ、共和党の主張した「ファミリー・バリュー」が失われ、社会が大きく変化していることにアメリカの大衆が戸惑いを感じていることは事実でしょう。良きにつけ悪しきにつけ、こうした価値観が論議される背景には、犯罪の増加や教育の問題、人々の疎外などといったアメリカ社会の抱える深刻な問題があることは否めないようです。

social problems. The epitome of "family values" was the traditional American family: a hardworking, pious father and mother with children who respect their parents, attend school, and actively participate in community work. The break-down of the family was seen as the key to the run-down state of education, juvenile crime, and the degeneration of the community.

But the theme of "family values" also became the target of criticism: people said it was out of touch with reality, enforced old values, and ran counter to ideas of gender equality—women should work on equal terms in society, and not just live to be mothers.

Other people criticized the simple-minded advocacy of family values as a vain attempt to turn back the clock and put the lid on the real problems in American society.

What is clear from all these differing opinions is that the great majority of American people felt disorientation in a society that was rapidly changing. They felt they were losing the "family values" the Republicans advocated. Putting aside questions of worth, such discussion surrounding "family values" highlights the most serious problems facing American society today: the increase in crime, problems in education, rising disparity of wealth and social alienation.

Q アメリカでの家庭崩壊の現状はどのようになっていますか?

アメリカでの家庭崩壊の現状を最も端的に示しているのが高い離婚率ではないでしょうか。2014年のアメリカ政府の統計によれば、婚姻率（人口1000人あたりの婚姻数）が6.9で、離婚率が3.2となっています。すなわち、こうした傾向は80年代から変わっていませんから、大まかにいえば約2組に1組が離婚していることになります。

従って、2人の親の元で育てられなかった子供が大変多いのです。なぜ離婚率が高いのかという背景には多くの理由が考えられます。アメリカ社会が豊かになり家族が全員で家庭を守っていく必要がなくなり、女性もどんどん社会に進出するようになったのもその理由の1つでしょう。また、元来自らの意志を主張し、貫いてゆくことを良しとする社会環境が、夫婦間の問題を解決するためにはうまく作用しないのかもしれません。

Q What is the real status of the breakdown of the family in the US?

The high divorce rate is probably the most clearest indication of the breakdown of the family in America. According to statistics in 2014, rates of marriage (rate per 1,000 total population) was 6.9 while almost 3.2 out of every 1,000 people got divorced. This trend has continued since the 1980s—which means, roughly speaking, that half the number of couples who marry later divorce.

As a result, many children are not raised by dual-parent families. Many reasons are conceivable for the high divorce rate. One of them may be women's advancement in society, and an increasing affluence making it less necessary for a family to stick together. There is also a general tendency to give great value to self-assertion, which does not necessarily work in the context of marriage.

人と自然

Q アメリカ人にとっての自然とはどのようなものですか？

アメリカ人は、新大陸に移住してこのかた、常に自然と戦い、それを克服しながら国土を広げ、農地を開き、鉄道を敷設してきました。自然をいかにコントロールするかということは、アメリカ人が常に課題としてきたことで、そうした中から物質文明への信奉や科学万能の考えがアメリカに広がりました。

この考え方は、いかに自然と自らを融合させるかというテーマを追いかけ、自然と共に生きることから独自の価値観を生み出してきたアジア諸国の価値観とは対照的なものといえそうです。

しかし、最近の自然環境の破壊の進行や飽食などによる人々の健康問題がクローズアップされる中、アメリカでは自然を支配しようという振り子が逆に振れ、既に何年にもわたって、自然保護と環境保全を求めた運動が全米で推進されているのも事実です。こうした運動が、さらには絶滅の危機に瀕した動植物への保護運動、有機農法や自然食品への回帰現象を生み出し、現在ではそれが大きな流れともなっています。

ヨセミテ国立公園の渓谷

国立公園と国立野生生物保護区を

People and Nature

Q What does nature mean to Americans?

In general, ever since they immigrated to the New World, Americans have fought against nature, conquered it, expanded frontiers, cultivated land, and laid railways. How to control nature was their perpetual preoccupation, which developed into a belief in material civilization and the science-is-everything attitude.

Such a stance is in contradiction to various countries in Asia, where people seek instead to merge themselves in nature, and where a particular value of coexistence with nature has arisen.

However, as the environment in America has suffered increasing devastation, and more attention has been given to health problems such as obesity, a shift has occurred in people's attitude toward nature. For years now there have been nationwide—and now worldwide—movements for environmental protection and preservation. These movements have led to the protection of endangered fauna and flora, and a widescale return to organic agriculture and consumption of natural foods.

It is worth remembering that it was the U.S. that

最初に作ったのはアメリカであることも覚えてお
きましょう。アメリカでは、学校が休みに入ると、
家族で国立公園を訪れるのは今でも人気なのです。

Q アメリカでは環境汚染はどのように抑制されているの ですか？

　身近なケースでいえば、庭に積もった落ち葉を
燃やすことを禁止したり、釣りをするときに許可
証の取得を義務づけ、釣って家庭に持ち帰ること
のできる魚介類やそのサイズまで細かく指定して
いる町や州まで、アメリカには環境保護のための
様々な法律が制定されています。

　とはいえ、アメリカの環境汚染は場所によって
は未だに深刻です。例えばロサンゼルスなどは、
スモッグのひどいときは、あたかも霧にでも覆わ
れたかのように町が霞んで見えます。こうした環
境を改善しようと、カリフォルニアでは常に強い
規制を盛り込んだ法律が検討されています。例え
ば、乗用車の量を減らすため、人と相乗りをして
いる車を優先的に通すレーンを高速道路に設けた
りといった規制もその例の1つです。また、企業
も環境にやさしい製品を造ったり、包装を簡易に
したりと、環境問題に取り組んでいることをPRの
道具にしたりしています。

　こうした官民一体の努力に加え、環境保護を訴

pioneered the creation of National Parks and National Wildlife Reserves, and it is still a favorite outing during school holidays for families to visit one of the National Parks.

Q What are the environmental pollution regulations in the US?

Various laws have been established in the US for environmental protection. To take one example, in some communities and states bonfires in one's yard are prohibited. One must get permission to fish, and there are limitations on the amount of fish and shellfish one can catch and take home.

Nonetheless, serious environmental pollution exists in some places in the US. For example, Los Angeles can become so laden with heavy smog that it sometimes appears to be covered in fog. The California government is forever trying out new laws and legal restrictions in order to remedy this problem. One such regulation set up carpool lanes giving priority to vehicles shared by two or more passengers, in an attempt to decrease the number of vehicles on the freeways. Companies also make pro-environmental products or simplified packages as part of their marketing strategies.

In addition to these joint efforts on the part of

える世論もアメリカでは大変強く、そうした動き
がさらに政府の政策決定に大きな影響を与えてい
るのです。2008年の大統領選挙戦で、オバマ政権
は、環境に対する政策や業界についてのキャンペー
ンまで行ったのです。

とはいえ、すでに述べたように、トランプ政権
は大統領戦のキャンペーン中に、前政権の推進し
てきた環境政策の多くを取りやめるか、その動き
を鈍らせると発表しました。今後、どのような流
れになるのか、見守っていくしかないでしょう。

ただ、そうはいってもそれではどこまで環境問
題を優先し、便利で快適な生活を抑制するかとな
ると、賛否両論で、こうしたことが、カリフォル
ニアなどでのさらに強い環境規制の法律の通過が
見送られたりという結果につながっています。

世界で最も多く自動車や飛行機が使用され、様々
なものが消費されているアメリカにとって、環境
問題に本気で取り組むことは、自らの生活の在り
方までも考え直さなければならない複雑な問題で
もあるのです。

Q　なぜアメリカ人はイルカや鯨を大切にするのですか？

鯨は乱獲で、頭数が激減し、捕鯨を禁止する国
際条約が締結されましたが、アメリカでは、そう

the government and the public, general support for environmental protection is very strong in the US, and exerts a large influence in government policymaking. The Obama Administration even campaigned on the development of green policies and industries during the presidential election of 2008.

As noted, however, the Trump Administration came in on a campaign promise to weaken or even reverse many of the environmental policies of previous administrations. Time will tell whether this really happens.

Even so, opinion varies as to how far environmental issues should be given priority, especially when policies threaten a convenient and comfortable lifestyle—as seen in California cases where bills with strong restrictions are often shelved.

The US has the largest number of planes and cars in the world, and the nation is a consumer of diverse goods. To face up to the environmental problem squarely means to reconsider the country's entire lifestyle.

Q Why do Americans feel so much affection for dolphins and whales?

An international treaty to prohibit whaling was established when the number of whales in the world

した保護運動をする中で鯨自体が自然保護のシンボル的な存在になったのです。それはイルカについてもいえることで、高等な頭脳を持つとされるイルカの物語がテレビやアニメで紹介され、イルカは海の人気者として注目を集めました。

　実はアメリカも昔は捕鯨大国でした。特に19世紀の中頃はアメリカの捕鯨船は世界を航海し、そうした捕鯨船の寄港する港を獲得することも、ペリーが幕末の日本に開国を求めた理由の１つでした。

　ただ、アメリカ人は食用ではなく、鯨からとれる脂をろうそくの原料として使用していたのです。従って、電気がお目見得すれば、捕鯨を行う必要はなくなったわけで、その後長い間、鯨はアメリカ人にとってはそれほど縁のある動物ではなくなりました。それだけに捕鯨の禁止に対しても抵抗なく賛成できたのでしょう。

　現在、アメリカでは鯨とイルカは動物愛護と環境保全のシンボルとして定着して、捕鯨の是非を問うこと自体がタブー視されているようなところがあるようです。

decreased dramatically due to unrestrained hunting. During the whale protection campaign, the whale became a symbol of wildlife protection in general. The same is true of the dolphin. Animated films and TV programs on dolphins that showed their advanced intelligence made the dolphin a popular ocean creature.

In fact, whale hunting was once carried out by the US, particularly in the mid-nineteenth century, when US whaling ships sailed the world. One of the reasons Perry asked Japan to open the country was to gain access to Japanese ports for American ships to harbor.

Americans used whale oil for making candles, not for food. Once electricity was invented, therefore, the need to catch whales disappeared, and whales became relatively unimportant for them. They thus had no objection to the prohibition of whaling.

Whales and dolphins have gained the status of symbols of animal protection and environmental preservation in the US today. Raising any question about the appropriateness of whaling restrictions is almost a taboo subject.

あとがき

　日本とアメリカとは切っても切れない関係にあります。

　それは、否定できない事実ですし、現実です。

　まえがきでも触れましたが、そんなアメリカが今変化しようとしています。きっと本書を２年後に読み返すと、そこにさらに加筆しなければならない重要なテーマがでてきていることでしょう。

　今まで世界で何かがおきると、人々が常にアメリカに流れ込んできました。例えば、ベトナム戦争が終わり、ベトナムが共産党政権によって統一されたとき、南ベトナムに住んでいた人々が難民としてボートに乗って国を離れ、アメリカにやってきました。今、アメリカ各地にリトルサイゴンという街があり、ベトナム系の人々が暮らしている背景はそこにあります。

　そして現在、中東の混乱で多くの人がボートに乗ってヨーロッパに逃れています。その波はなんらかの形でアメリカにも到達するはずです。

　160年前には、当時イギリス領だったアイルランドから、飢饉や圧政に苦しむ人々が大量にアメリカにやってきました。こうした例をあげればきりがありません。

　アメリカが世界と関わらなければならない現実は、単にアメリカが強国だからではなく、こうした世界からの移民が国民となっているからに他なりません。

　そんなアメリカが、これから同じように世界に関わってゆくことができるのか。また、中国やロシアが世界の新しい超大国として影響力

を増している現在、戦後のように、アメリカが自由主義社会のリーダーとして、強い力を発揮できるのか。そのベースとなる経済や社会構造が状況に対応できるように歪みなく変化できるのか。課題は多く残されています。

　アメリカには常に貧富の差がありました。新しくやってくる移民の多くは貧しく、豊かさを求めて地位を築くのに必死でした。

　しかし、貧富の差や格差での不公平を最近感じているのは、古くからアメリカに住む白人系の人々なのです。今回の大統領選挙でドナルド・トランプ氏が選ばれた原因であったともいわれています。

　従って、アメリカはこれから過去に経験をしたことのない社会変化の波に見舞われるかもしれないのです。

　それは、日本もその波の影響を受けることは間違いありません。

　ですから、ぜひこれからもアメリカの動向を注視したいものです。本書が、そうした一助になれれば幸いです。

装　　幀：岩目地英樹（コムデザイン）
英語編集協力：Leza Lowitz
　　　　　　David Satterwhite

日英対訳 アメリカQ&A

2017年2月7日　第1刷発行

著　者　山久瀬　洋二

発行者　浦　　晋　亮

発行所　**IBCパブリッシング株式会社**
　　　　〒162-0804 東京都新宿区中里町29番3号 菱秀神楽坂ビル9F
　　　　Tel. 03-3513-4511　Fax. 03-3513-4512
　　　　www.ibcpub.co.jp

印刷所　中央精版印刷株式会社

© 2017 IBC Publishing
Printed in Japan

落丁本・乱丁本は、小社宛にお送りください。送料小社負担にてお取り替えいたします。
本書の無断複写（コピー）は著作権法上での例外を除き禁じられています。

ISBN978-4-7946-0458-3

本書の英文は、2011年に小社から刊行されたラダーシリーズ『America FAQ』を
増補・改訂し、再編集したものです。

English Conversational Ability Test
国際英語会話能力検定

● E-CATとは…
英語が話せるようになるための
テストです。インターネット
ベースで、30分であなたの発
話力をチェックします。

www.ecatexam.com

● iTEP®とは…
世界各国の企業、政府機関、アメリカの大学
300校以上が、英語能力判定テストとして採用。
オンラインによる90分のテストで文法、リー
ディング、リスニング、ライティング、スピー
キングの5技能をスコア化。iTEP®は、留学、就
職、海外赴任などに必要な、世界に通用する英
語力を総合的に評価する画期的なテストです。

www.itepexamjapan.com